P. MANSELL JONES
(1889-1968)

HOW
THEY EDUCATED JONES

by

P. MANSELL JONES

with a Foreword by
Eugène Vinaver

CARDIFF
UNIVERSITY OF WALES PRESS
1974

© Miss Annie Elizabeth Jones

ISBN O 7083 0442 7

PRINTED IN WALES
BY D. BROWN AND SONS LTD.,
EASTGATE PRESS, COWBRIDGE, GLAM.

CONTENTS

FOREWORD

L I K E most great men Mansell Jones was unware of his greatness. He looked upon himself as a very ordinary worker in his chosen field and thought he was lucky to be allowed to explore it at leisure. Expressions of admiration for his work as a writer and scholar seemed to puzzle him; he responded to them not with the customary words of gratitude, but with a somewhat incredulous 'I see'. When the University of Manchester offered him the newly established Chair of Modern French Literature (he was until then Professor of French at Bangor) he wrote to the Vice-Chancellor saying that he was 'tempted to think seriously of accepting if the post was really within his competence'. The University, he thought, ought to know 'the limits of his resources'. And when he finally came and assumed —very diffidently—the responsibilities of the new Chair he had obviously no idea what his presence meant to those of us who were to be privileged to work with him for five golden years. We used to say that there was a special look of happiness in the eyes of those who had just been talking to 'P.M.' as he was known to us all, but he himself was convinced that what he gave was not worth much, that it was at most—in his own words—a matter of 'helping better men to write better books'.

Interest in oneself and a certain degree of confidence in one's own achievement are the obvious pre-requisites of any autobiographical project, and this is why Mansell Jones could never have written a proper autobiography. The manuscript he left bearing the title *How They Educated Jones* could not be so described. While *they*— those who educated him—are firmly placed in the centre of the work, not much is said about Jones himself. The book is less of a record of his formative years than a work of meditation. It is also a piece of imaginative writing of unusual quality, which cannot fail to become part of English literature.

The background of it all is the British academic scene of the first quarter of this century. University programmes at the time when Mansell Jones was a student were considered daring if they contained any reference to literature—English or foreign—later than 1880. An academic subject was supposed to be something which

had ceased to live, and it was natural that once this principle was accepted literature should have been taught in a way that had no relation to literary experience. Two other factors helped to dehumanize the study of texts in modern European languages. One was the conviction that in order to qualify as a serious University discipline what was known as 'philology' had to be interpreted not in the original humanistic sense, but in the characteristically British sense of a non-literary pursuit—a self-imposed restriction of meaning prompted no doubt by the will to survive in a *milieu* where any other conception of literary scholarship might have been thought frivolous. Mansell Jones was exposed to one of the worst forms of this anomaly in his student days at Aberystwyth when the whole of the *Chanson de Roland* was presented to him as a series of curiously deformed Latin vowels and consonants which it was his business as a student to sort out and trace to their roots. The study of literature as a coherent discourse did eventually find its way into University curricula, but only through the adoption by modern linguists of another equally strange anomaly—the so-called *explication de texte*. Like so many things imported from France it won general recognition before anyone had troubled to inqure what its original purpose was and what kind of audience it was intended for, with the result that what was originally an exercise in mental discipline for schoolchildren was raised to the dignity of an academic pursuit. Courteline's delightful sketch, *Mon petit frère*, is a skit—alarmingly close to the original—on the kind of unconscious distortion of great poetry that went on, and is still going on, in French *lycées* under the aegis of 'training in method'. What Courteline did not know was that while he was writing his sketch the dialogue which he ridiculed was being practised in all seriousness in some of the great seats of learning across the Channel.

To a writer and critic like Mansell Jones both these approaches, the etymological and the rhetorical, naturally seemed meaningless. Feeling as he did the need for a radical change from his exposure to both of them, he turned his attention to contemporary literature and so became the founder in England of modern French literary studies. In complete disregard of the chronological limit set by University programmes he wrote his first book on a contemporary Belgian poet, Emile Verhaeren, and when he went to France to

complete his studies it was again to explore the modern field—a region totally unknown to his elders in University departments. Nor was it to them that he went for advice. The one valuable piece of guidance he received came from Ezra Pound who encouraged him to go in search, not of other professors of literature, but of living poets. There followed a visit to Paris which the young traveller described in unforgettable terms, combining humorous *reportage* with a meaningful record of an inspired pilgrimage. His subsequent writings on modern French poetry, including many luminous pages of his *Baudelaire*, were directly or indirectly an outcome of these early exploits of an adventurous mind. The present volume only takes us to the threshold of a very active literary life, but it ends on a significantly dramatic note—with a symbolic escape 'into the Florentine dusk' where art had lived for centuries and was still a living thing. Life for Mansell Jones, before and after this escape, was but a quest for living values—and a passionate revolt in the name of their integrity.

Nobody could have looked less like a rebel than this unfailingly courteous Edwardian *universitaire* whose urbane, yet vigorous speech was the essence of civilized elegance. He never spoke disparagingly of anyone, with the exception of his Aberystwyth Professor who appears anonymously in these pages. He showed nothing but respect for people who spent their lives doing things which from his point of view were utterly useless. An occasional phrase, a carefully worded image was all that he would venture by way of criticizing other people; but such phrases and images were devastating in their effects. 'The essence often escapes the hand that traps the influence'; is this not the most striking and complete judgment ever passed on a whole school of academic criticism? Among the people with whom Mansell Jones spent his academic life there was hardly anyone of whom this could not have been said, and hardly anyone who could have understood what was meant by 'essence'. Few things are more distressing than the reading of reviews of his *Assault on French Literature*—one of the great books of our time which the learned journals in their innocence left to the tender mercies of reviewers who from the nature of things could not have known what the book was about. They enjoyed their condescending irrelevances. 'Les nains', as Flaubert once said, 'aiment à voir les géants raccourcis'.

Far from resenting the incongruity of the situation, Mansell Jones was only too ready to admit that what he was involved in was not really 'scholarship', but something different: a type of work which had possibly less right to a place in the academic world than some of the more pedestrian, abundantly documented studies on topics of doubtful significance. He certainly never claimed a superior rank for his kind of learning—the learning beautifully illustrated by his *French Introspectives*, his *Verhaeren* and his *Baudelaire*, all of them master-pieces of perceptive criticism, free from any *a priori* view of what literature should be and inspired by an infectiously vivid, and yet superbly controlled aesthetic experience.

If Mansell Jones was too modest a man to write an autobiography, no one will deny that everything he wrote, including this book, is a true image of what was most profoundly personal in him. Every page is an unintentional confession, a page out of a diary which was never meant to be one, but which precisely for this reason is a more truthful record of the writer's self than most books deliberately planned as autobiographies. 'Qui ne vit aucunement à autrui, ne vit guère à soi'. This dictum of Montaigne, which Mansell Jones him-self quotes in concluding his book on French introspectives, is perhaps one of the best formulations of his own mode of thought. He saw Montaigne emerging greater in retrospect and superior in wisodm 'because he looked both ways', because of the wonderful balance he had achieved of 'inner and outer cultivation', even when he had abandoned any conscious quest for self. And this perhaps is the real and the most vital meaning of Mansell Jones's own explorations.

In the form in which he left the book there was room for some rearrangement if it was to retain the proportions which it was originally meant to have. It contained material for two different works: the memoirs of the author's childhood in Wales and the story of 'how they educated him'. Of the former the present volume reproduces the two essential chapters, leaving the rest for a separate publication which, it is hoped, will not be long delayed. The only other departure from the manuscript as the author left it is the position of what is now Chapter I and what was originally the final chapter. I must take full responsibility for what seemed to me a means of bringing out at the very outset something which sets the tone and the character of the entire work. This chapter is not unlike a portrait

facing the title-page. It is not part of the narrative; but it is part of
the man himself—an inner reflection of the values to which his whole
existence was dedicated. It may well be that these profoundly
personal pages will be still better understood in the light of what
follows, which is all the more reason to read them first. The rest of
the book is a commentary on them, and an indispensable one, but
even the best commentary is only effective if we have first read the
work commented upon. As T. S. Eliot has it, 'our first reading of
a work of literature which we do not understand is itself the
beginning of understanding', for 'understanding begins in the
sensibility'. This is what Mansell Jones himself believed to be the
right approach to literature, and this is how, I feel, his own writings
should be read.

Eugène Vinaver

PREFACE

I HAVE never kept a regular diary of moods and meditations. But between forty and fifty years ago I became interested in examples of the French personal genre, the *journal intime*, and no doubt the example of Amiel in particular and later of André Gide encouraged, though they did not originate, the practice of writing down detached impressions alternating with chance quotations from more or less eminent masters of thought and expression. From time to time a simple experience or a natural scene or perhaps a reminiscence of something that had happened in school, in college or at home would become clear and insistent enough to get itself recorded; and it was more the recording of the subject and the cultivation of a style (about which one used to hear much in the form of injunction but little by way of correction or advice) that helped to ingrain the habit. All this was spontaneous and amateurish.

Gradually it became obvious that certain topics—nature (the spectacle, not the science), school and university life, snippets of secondhand literary appreciation and bits of philosophical and religious wisdom—kept recurring for annotation more persistently than others, and that vague relationships—a link or two of cohesion or the stimulus of a contrast—were springing up between them. Outlines of a personal education were coming into view.

A first draft of these outlines I called 'Romantic Education'. The epithet was adopted not merely as an echo caught from the debate between the champions of Neo-Classicism and the defenders of Romanticism that raged in France and England after the first world war. It was rather in the sense of 'panlyrical' that the epithet seemed to suit so much of the education I had received. Or should I not confess that the word 'romantic' fitted only too well those elements of the curriculum which I preferred and tended to concentrate on from the secondary stage onward?

Gradually as the once strident dialogue between the critics became less intense, the consciousness of a more intimate contrast increased between what I now prefer to call the systematic education, with its professional and administrative paraphernalia, and the kind of

education received direct from the modest social and domestic milieux in which my early years had been spent. Here was a contrast infinitely better worth working out, if only I could improvise the tools and find time for the job.

Not long ago, the late Dr. Ernest Jones, an infinitely abler Welshman than the subject of this record, described himself in his autobiography as having been 'a youth who.....had no special endowment of facility, aptitude or mental power'. He had to work hard for everything he acquired, and although outwardly merry and friendly, inwardly, he says, he was over-earnest for his age. I feel I could appropriate most, if not all, of these words. Merry I could never claim to have been, and what humour I have reflects the gay and genial spirits that have flourished around me. But over-earnestness was certainly in my line.

Of conspicuous deficiencies for this self-appointed task I must confess at least two. Here another of Dr. Jones's remarks comes in useful. References to health and sickness should, he thought, be made in autobiographies, and he complained that obituaries in *The Times* never tell what people die of. He admitted, however, that no one could be more boring than the person who indulges in the deadliest of fads,—talking of his ailments. And since I have a malady of long standing I had better assure the prospective reader that he is not going to be involved in an invalid's *journal intime*—and for rather a hard reason. It has beggared the nomenclature of the medical profession to find a name for what I ail from. Well over fifty years ago an excellent G.P. passed me his medical dictionary with the suggestion that I should search its columns for an identification of my complaint. Less than a decade ago an intelligent young house physician sat on my bedside in a great city hospital and divulged that he did not think a diagnosis could ever be found. The question of the moment, however, is not the name and nature of certain 'psychosomatic symptoms' (to give them a vague salute) but to ask how far they have affected the writer of this book. Somewhere in his volumes of truth and error Proust puts his finger on the right view. I will gloss his verdict thus: the 'secret' of a complaint is not in its symptoms but in the person who is suffering from them. How far, then, does ill-health disqualify the author from claiming to represent the average studious youth of his time? In one important sphere of their interests he could not, obviously,

stake a claim: my story shows no reference to sport. This gap will, I hope, be accepted as a sign of personal disability, not as a failure to appreciate the importance of games in education or to ignore the zest they add to existence. Playing a lazy round of tennis, manœuvring an old Austin along country lanes and being warned by approaching telegraph poles not to gaze too long over the hills and far away, or manipulating a couple of light leather cases between foreign railway stations and the first cheap hotel in sight—these mark my limits in manly exercises; though I must allow that in my prime I climbed a mountain slope or two beyond the reach of the funicular.

A far more serious obstacle to evoking the past than a lack of participation in some of life's active diversions must now be confessed. How can a man hope to win confidence in the record of his experiences if he had to begin by confessing one of the worst defects of an uncertain memory—a sub-normal power of verbal recollection? 'And you a language teacher!' the reader may interpose. Alas, to teach anything strictly dependent on correct wording has been a constant and sometimes a heart-rending strain. Yet I have some kind of memory, as I hope will be conceded. I will call it a memory for impressions and will rate my quota of impressionability a little above the average degree, though far below an exceptional endowment. Impressions of the kind that remain with me depend mainly on sight, easily the strongest of my senses. Most of my recollections come back as things or persons seen, a few with precision, the majority in salient outline. But that none of them could remain bright for ever becomes clear when I turn to the earliest of those preserved in the following pages and realize that I could not now recall them in the detail with which they were at first set down.

I take no pride in declaring that I have rarely succeeded in refreshing myself with light or frivolous forms of writing. This, however, may be thought a vain boast when I commit my last act of self-betrayal. One big temptation that I have never yet learnt to avoid has been the lure of secondary literature of the type of commentary and the seductions of modern criticism and elegant scholarship. The agreeable tones of Connolly, Mortimer and Philip Toynbee I rarely fail to catch, mingling with St. Peter's chimes as they ring out over our ancient borough on Sunday mornings; and

there are other more august voices in whose wisdom I revel surreptitiously with a rustic, reprehensible enthusiasm.

                                                              P.M.J.

Carmarthen, April 1967.

CHAPTER ONE

NATURE AND EXPRESSION

I CAN distinguish in others, and have myself known, two species of reaction to the beauty of the world. One is a sensitiveness to what may be called the picturesque, a pure or flat response of the eye, and almost alone of that organ, increasing in vividness and subtlety according to the sensibility of the seer. It is the common property of nature lovers, observant tramps abroad, and of many poets. By far the greater number of French poets seem to have responded to nature in this way. Wordsworth himself confessed to have started with

> a feeling and a love,
> That had no need of a remoter charm,
> By thought supplied, or any interest
> Unborrowed from the eye.

The other is a more profound mode of reaction easier to illustrate than to describe. It is commoner among Teutonic and Anglo-Saxon poets. Wordsworth is here the great example. Richard Jefferies is one of many lesser writers, in whom I found it developed to a major degree. I can believe that it is by no means rare among people who love nature. But it came as a surprise, some years ago, to discover that not everyone who talked of nature with enthusiasm, who was fond of walking the countrysides and of observing natural scenes, was having the type of experience I am trying to distinguish. In all probability theirs was the more superficial or less specific reaction, which is now all that is left to me of what has been perhaps the most profound mood I have known. But now I am faced with the difficulty of explaining or analysing from memory this rarer experience.

It was in my case a gift of sunshine and stillness. The noisier moods of nature, however impressive, did not bring it. But vistas of mountain or shore, sweeps of variegated or undulating landscape altitudes or declivities, wherever there was depth or distance, size variety or fecundity; or, on the other hand, massive uniformity and extensive barrenness, mystery, vagueness or gloom—provided

that the air was calm and temperate, conducive to oblivion of distracting sensations such as those produced by chill or fatigue or blustering winds or any noise but the rhythm of an ebbing tide— these brought the change, a kind of conscious swoon, a soft release, a benediction bestowed by the aspect of tranquil or tremendous things,

> Until, the breath of this corporeal frame
> And even the motion of our human blood
> Almost suspended, we are laid asleep
> In body, and become a living soul.

I remember having seen the sea, the sky and the shore radiant and flashing in the sun. It must have been during one of the summer sojourns of our childhood at a village in the bay. The circumstances are effaced. There remain only two impressions, one of the radiance of the sky, the wet sand and the sea; the other of a vague, enormous, indescribable feeling. When I apply the analysis of maturity it is as if, standing on the sand near the sea and plunging my eyes into the threefold radiance, I stood on the threshold of an experience entirely different from anything known before, an experience of immense and shining joy, through which, transported, I should participate in the radiant life of sky, shore and sea. Now as I write, I feel a ghost faltering on the frontiers of that moment of potential ecstasy. Distanced by time and space, the vision represents me, a black spot lost in the centre of the immense illumination. I have turned my back on it and stand facing the valley that narrows upon a little town higher up the stream, my native town with its modest beauty and its mortal ennui.

When I compare the type of experience this memory illustrates with other absorbing experiences of my youth, I find that neither concentration on religious thoughts, nor efforts at moral improvement, nor even the exercise of prayer with which I struggled for many years, ever brought an equal awareness of having approached a state of mind which, for want of a better term, I will call mystical.

My pious endeavours had cultivated a sense of moral values and had inspired a desire, more than a determination, to live the good life, the religion of my youth having been essentially a kind of idealized morality, a dynamic urging to deeds of service and to self-improvement, or a brake, curbing healthy as well as unhealthy tendencies. The mood which nature gave was passive. It pointed to

nothing conscious, purposive or obvious beyond itself. It was capable of opening an abyss of pessimism under one's feet, but it could also be immensely elevating and act as a catharsis. At times it seemed a realization of absolute beauty superior to all forms created by man, though not spiritual in the sense of being symbolic of anything higher. Autonomous, primordial, everlasting, yet for the spectator ephemeral, perceived only to pass with desperate, delicious fleetingness. For a moment one had been part of the unity of nature, glimpsed as universal beauty. Religion pure and undefiled was a composite experience compared with this inalienable absolute.

Sometimes a common object would stand out in a special light and attract one in a peculiar way. A green ash sapling drenched with sunset, upright at crossroads near my home and fixed preternaturally still against the soft azure sky; or another young ash I saw in a garden at Aberfeldy one gloomy morning, fragile but motionless against the mirk of a wide grey declivity—such objects could hold my attention until something momentarily happened to them or to me.

I should explain that I have had no experience of the kind called 'queer', nor have I much interest in them. I consider myself, as I grow older, to be hopelessly rational. Without, as an offset, being able to flatter myself on possessing Gautier's vision of the brilliant, obdurate, inexhaustibly novel concrete—*le rêve du réel* he called it in a phrase I find suspicious,—what I see are just stocks and stones and the common colours and shapes of such common things. And I have wished not to betray these things by extraneous images or to attempt to suggest them by vague metaphors or symbols which might stand for something finer but not for these very things.

I have no taste for the fantastic and am impatient of visions. Never have I wanted to see the world more beautiful, more wonderful or more fanciful than I find it on a bright day. I am thus a prisoner of the real, by which I mean the common world as I suppose it appears to most people who trouble to look at it. So much a prisoner that at times I feel it pressing, obtruding, clamouring, around. My cranium might be an eggshell with the feet of the world's traffic thudding over it in nailed boots.

Judge then my relief to find, without conscious artifice, this green sapling with Aberfeldy in a dip behind, on a palpably damp morning, becoming something *other*, momentarily changed

into—what? No burning bush, you may believe! I can only describe the change as something intimating the blessed *unreality* of the world I hold so real.

I cannot claim that I too have been in Arcady. But when people were not passing I have cautiously snatched my private view of the common, startling loveliness of earth. And I have doubted if anything could be more perfect and have wondered whether, if just this could be secured or perpetuated, one would not have heart's desire and the sum of all good.

Preoccupation with nature and doubtless the mood itself which was her secret boon were stimulated and accentuated by what I knew of the English Romantic poets and of writers derivative from them. My acquaintance with their works was neither broad nor thorough. But I must have read enough to get them into my blood, though I doubt whether I could recall correctly three consecutive lines from any of their writings. It is characteristic, I think, that the Romantics appealed to me paramountly by the nature side of their work; to a much lesser extent by its sentimental or erotic side. Most of my own sentiment was diverted from normal channels into nature worship. All the verse I read was lyrical. The best of it lies within the last two sections of Palgrave's *Golden Treasury*. I need not emphasize the emotional quality of this kind of literature, its lack of specific intellectual stimulus. At best it produced deep reverie; it was obviously not conducive to hard thinking. In saying this I make no pretence at objective criticism. I simply desire to show the close connection between my taste in natural scenery and the moods it produced, on one hand, and on the other, the powerful ferment that proceeded from the quintessence of lyricism I was then imbibing in pure, if not extensive, draughts.

Palgrave, I think, apologized for omitting from his collection the *Lines* Wordsworth wrote above Tintern Abbey, and I feel I should apologize for calling them my favourite of all poems since, so far in life, I have been unable to look at them critically. This is no doubt an admission of weakness. But for me Wordsworth's poem remains unimpeachably beyond criticism or praise one of the peaks of experience. 'Peaks' is not the right word; 'depths' is not much better, but I will leave it at that.

Looking at country through the eyes of the poets and at poetry in the light of nature, I began to make private efforts at rivalling the

masters—private, not surreptitious, because there was no need to conceal experiments in versifying in milieux that were not alienated from the arts in the way comparable milieux would risk being today. All I can recall of the earliest of my experiments is that they were inspired by natural themes, were written in pentameters either unrhymed or in quatrains, and were feeble enough to dissatisfy even the complacent standards of my embryonic taste. Facility in any form of expression has always been a remote danger. But I confess to having had a desperate persistence in the direction of an obscure, and doubtless a much mistaken goal.

Psychologists would have something to say on this topic. An impulse towards compensation must have underlain it. I was sometimes half conscious that the lure of self-expression appealed to me vaguely as creating an opportunity for a kind of self-justification. That, however, came later. The original impulse was a response to stimuli. The sporadic results of my literary endeavours often displeased me so much that I would leave the "lyre" untouched for long periods, with a proper determination not to repeat my follies. Then, one day or another, a common scene, a sunset or a sea view, would somehow be getting itself recorded in trite poetic formulas, patiently fashioned into a sonnet as obvious in feeling and imagery as it was stereotyped in form. This vague, desultory experimentation went on for some years, producing nothing but a sense of mild elation, followed by its corrective of mild depression. The mischief was that, not having been born a poet, I could not persuade myself to abandon poetic form. Meanwhile it would be no exaggeration to admit that to compose a decent paragraph of discursive, as opposed to "poetic" prose was quite beyond me. Apart from a few letters, I had no occasion or cause to write anything in the pedestrian medium. The only essays prescribed in the English course I had taken at College had been those imposed in the Examination room.

My experiments in trying to capture the mood met the doom that few of its votaries have been able to avoid. But as some of the experiences accompanying these efforts count among my most picturesque memories, I must attempt to describe one or two of them here.

During the summer of 1914, in response to an invitation from a 'Scots' uncle, I spent a few weeks at his home in the heart of Aberdeenshire. Ivor, my father's younger brother, was an excise

officer or "gauger" at the remote distillery of Glendronnach which
had given its name to a blend of Grant's whisky, honourably
mentioned by George Saintsbury in his *Notes on a Cellar Book*.
The prospect was one of being buried for a month in highland
country thirty miles away from the nearest town of any size with
not even a steeple in sight—nothing in fact to relieve the bare hills
and rough walled fields but the heavy grey roofs of the low distillery
buildings.   For me, however, there were two distractions that
absorbed most of the time I spent there. One of them was unexpected.
My uncle's wife, who was old enough to have been my mother, I
discovered to be an attractive woman and the friendship that struck
up between us remained firm for the rest of her life.   She had a
strong fine face and her long exile in this remote parish had neither
hardened her character nor curbed her ready wit.   A week before
my arrival she had caught sight of the vicar looking over a wall as
she helped my uncle to dig up some potatoes in the close.   'Adam
and Eve in the garden,' he had blurted out playfully.   'And the
Old Gentleman outside,' she had responded.   My aunt was a
descendant of Rob Roy Macgregor and she humorously confided
to me that a few drops of blood of a runaway duchess of Sutherland
also coursed through her veins.

It required all the courage these forebears had transmitted for a
woman of spirit and intelligence to live uncomplainingly in that
northern fastness. One day my uncle didn't turn up for lunch. The
liquor whose quality he controlled had got the better of him. This,
I gathered, was a periodic occurrence which had for some years
prevented promotion to a brighter neighbourhood.   During such
lapses his placid temper could easily become ruffled, as when kissing
my aunt goodnight, I caused an infuriating *fracas* by upsetting a
glass jug of water she was carrying upstairs.   I prefer however to
associate my uncle with a less trivial incident: seeing him hollow
his hands round his mouth as he shouted across the fields: 'The
Germans are pouring into Belgium!'

Glendronnach, I have said, provided a couple of distractions that
made the time I spent there fly. The second can perhaps be guessed.
The distillery lies in a broad shallow valley sloping down from hills
of moderate height but rugged and unspoiled.   These I used to
climb, intent on noticing the shape of the land and the colours of
the sparse growths around.   Characteristically the natural objects

were perceived as emotional stimuli: the commonest of them remain in my mind as things seen and obscurely felt but not as things observed with any botanical or geological precision. Clusters of yellow ragwort lit up the stony turf and forced themselves on my attention. And the contrasts between them and the faint blue horizons beyond prompted jottings that were afterwards to be worked up into paragraphs of flat descriptive prose that strove to record things as I had found them, but for a touch of religious elevation that might work its way in at the end. Pressing on up the slopes I came upon something unexpected. A sunlit garden bright with fruit and flowers led to a filthy cottage and left so strong an impression of fascination and disgust that I tried, incongruously enough, to capture it in Whitmanian free verse. After much revision one or two of these efforts found their way later into Oxford periodicals. It was wartime and the editors must have been short of copy.

For solitude I have always had an impolite partiality, though I cannot endure it unravished for long. I have never been much disturbed by the presence of my fellows in places and on occasions when a romantic isolation would have been the appropriate setting. Nor has the imperturbable commonplace of my mind failed to react in the prescribed, or even in a personal, manner to one or other of the wonders of the world, before which it would have been more tactful to affect a *nil admirari* poise.

On a first visit to Geneva I had stayed on through uncertain weather, hoping to get a glimpse of Mont Blanc. One bright afternoon I thought I saw it. But in the evening my friends sympathetically intimated that the mountain's top had not been revealed and they advised me to try my chance with the Jungfrau as I returned home.

At Interlaken the atmosphere was still less propitious. A maid at the inn where I had spent the night assumed the role of my Genevan advisers. Surveying the heights from the door next morning, she pronounced a gloomy verdict which gave me regrets for the circuit I had made. I decided, however, to attempt the conventional tour of the Scheidegg and I joined a depressed party making for the funicular through a cold mist. The journey began, visibility improving a trifle as we ascended. After twenty minutes climb the small train turned sharply and a cry of surprise escaped us.

Above the mist an incredibly lofty slope, pitched at an impossible angle, glistened in sunlight with the warm smoothness of an arm gloved in white lifted against a clear morning sky. The effect of that suave cliff of warm whiteness soaring and shimmering in the azure was uncannily beautiful. The rest of the day was spent amid noble shapes and primary colours aloft. As we descended the valley that evening, the Virgin faded through gradations of crimson, rose and pink to a faint cadaverous green. All her aspects were ethereal. In death she was a fragile alabaster cone lit by an internal moon with that frigid glint of blue that shows at the edge of a crevice in the snows.

Ten years later I climbed the Brévent to stare at the mountain that had evaded me before. A couple of hours' ascent through the woods brought me to the ledge of sward which gives the panorama. There at last was the whole massif, peaks, *aiguilles*, glaciers, slopes of snow and pine, cabins, lawns, hotels and reservoirs cut out in exact circumstantiality of detail—a coloured contour map!

Through the long afternoon I sat watching wisps of silver fleece appear in mid-air, mount the higher slopes to evaporate before they reached the apices. I had watched this happen on that afternoon in the Oberland but with a difference. Cortes upon a peak in Darien had become Mark Twain on the Rhigi.

Had the mood been anything but a subjective delusion? If the mind had been alert enough when it was experienced, could one have penetrated to something beyond? Or was it in essence inconclusive? The more I examined not only my own experience but records of what I thought resembled it, the nearer I came to suspecting that, as a spiritual mode, nature was bankrupt. Had not her High Priest himself lamented the passing of the light? Coleridge's reminder rankled:

> . . . we receive but what we give,
> And in our life alone doth nature live.

But it was not until years later that, coming on a passage in *A l'ombre des jeunes filles en fleur*, I realized with sharp nostalgic poignancy the lure and emptiness of my youthful experiences.

Proust's hero is returning from Conqueville in Mme de Villeparisis's carriage when, at the sight of three trees standing back from the road, he is overwhelmed with a sense of happiness profound but not complete. As he looks at the trees his mind feels

that they are concealing something which it has not grasped. For that he should have been alone. He tries to abstract himself. 'I sat there thinking of nothing, then with my thoughts collected, compressed and strengthened I sprang farther forward in the direction of the trees, or rather in that inverse direction at the end of which I could see them growing within myself'. And again he feels behind them the same object known to him, yet vague, which he cannot bring nearer. Where had he looked at them before? Did they come from years so remote that the landscape which accompanied them had been entirely obliterated from memory? Were they not rather to be numbered among his dream landscapes: objectivisations presented in sleep of scenes that had puzzled him in daytime or reminiscences already worn and distant of last night's dream? Or had he never seen them before? Did they conceal beneath their surface, like the trees, like the tufts of grass that he had seen besides the Guermantes way, a meaning as obscure, as hard to grasp as in a far-off past, so that whereas they were pleading with him that he should master a new idea, he imagined that he had to identify something with memory? Presently at crossroads the carriage left them. It was bearing him away from what alone he believed to be true, what could have made him truly happy; it was like his life.

'I watched the trees gradually withdraw, waving their despairing arms, seeming to say to me: "What you fail to learn from us today you will never know. If you allow us to drop back into the hollow of this road from which we sought to raise ourselves up to you, a whole part of yourself which we were bringing to you will fall for ever into the abyss." And indeed, if in the course of time I did discover the kind of pleasure and of disturbance which I had just been feeling once again, and if one evening—too late, but then for all time—I fastened myself to it, of these trees themselves I was never to know what they had been trying to give me, nor where else I had seen them. And when, the road having forked and the carriage with it, I turned my back on them and ceased to see them, with Mme Villeparisis asking me what I was dreaming about, I was as wretched as though I had just lost a friend, had lied to myself, had broken faith with the dead or had denied my God'.

That passage has haunted me like certain developments in music, striving through repetition and modulation to reveal the mystery of

nature, wistfully investigating it as music seems at times to do, yet leaving it, as music ever does, no less remote after evocation. The secret was always to be divulged over the next hill: it would have whispered in one's ear had one been alone, had one waited longer, had one not turned a corner. It was like my life.

CHAPTER TWO

COLOURS OF CHILDHOOD

CARMARTHEN

SOMETIMES in December when the floods have subsided after long spells of rain, the sky over the valley can become serene and, of a winter's evening, the hills appear softly etched in brightness from the west. Looking north-east, the vista of river, fields and hills leads far off to the high line of the Vans. Across the head of the valley the Black Mountains extend, rising faintly to their greatest altitude, then dropping in a sheer cliff whose edge is now softened by distance and the failing light. The mildness of the rainy season has passed; the air is crisp and sharp and the distant range is already white with snow.

Behind the onlooker the early evening sun sinking beyond the town has suffused the scene with soft crimson and gold. But now the lengthening colours are fading progressively up the valley. Even the range ahead, losing line and mass, dissolves into the gathering obscurity. A moment or two more it lingers ghost-like on the horizon before its shape is quite effaced. Even now if you gaze fixedly into the hollow dusk there seem to emerge, only to recede again and again to emerge, the faintest silvery gleams. High in the clear sky the moon has risen unobserved. It hangs over the valley and is casting shimmers of evanescent silver on the hidden flanks of snow.

So in the vista of our memories the lineaments of our past lives flash and fade. Most of them we lose entirely. Others come back vividly etched by joy or pain. A few return etherealized by time and distance, hovering beyond precise recollection on the lost horizons of our fortuitous moods.

Back of all my memories looms an old door slanting in its frame and thickly corruscated with the clotted 'skins' of half-a-century's experiment in mixing and blending. The workshop door, upon whose variegated daubs and blisters the men tried their fresh colours, used to make me think of Joseph's coat, but that was a flattering association.

What it really resembled was a squalid patchwork quilt, hung
out to dry in the wretched little yard which with its uneven pavings,
traversed by an open gutter and shut in by high walls, was all there
was to be seen from our back windows except a geometrical piece of
sky and, over crowded roof-tops, the dormer windows of the Ivy
Bush Royal Hotel in Spilman Street.

Square Georgian houses wedged us in. Our front windows gave
upon a narrow street of them, superficially transformed into shops,
their plain façades and simple woodwork painted in sedate tones.
Lofty and impersonal, they seemed to impose upon us from across
the way, spurning the narrow muddy road, where rough-hewn
stones were strewn when the rains set in, to be crushed down by
the hoofs and wheels of a winter's traffic. When the rains set in
. . . but it was always raining. Children of the mist, we seem to have
passed from infancy to youth, from youth to adolescence, enmeshed,
immured in the fine reticulation of permanent rain. It soaked into our
clothes, seeped through our skins, penetrated our lungs, our hearts,
our brains. For weeks, for months, it would fall day and night,
softly, incessantly. The somnolent old town, the wistful valley would
be wrapt close in a vast blanket woven out at sea by the warm south-
wester. The clinging clouds might lift a little, the valley reappear
outlined in green and grey; then at either end its lines would blur,
they would fade out like thin green flames before the reinvasion of
sea-mist and more rain.

Always eager to overflow its banks, the sinuous river would creep
out in pale sheets over the marshes and the vale become an arm of
the sea thirty miles away when the windings were counted from its
parent body. Soon the lower roads are covered; boats pass along
with provisions; a plucky doctor's gig splashes through the mud.
Dwellers on the quay have moved to their attic storeys whence, often
enough, they watch their chattels swirl down-stream along with a
carcass or two swept off the meadows. The modernised castle, used
as a jail, looks the stern citadel it must often have been of old,
riding an inland sea, now intercepted only by the parapets of the
ancient bridge, sunk for the thousandth time beneath the flood.

Could this be, over again, what my first biblical lessons called the
Deluge? Hope went and came with the climatic changes. Just when
one felt the floods must mount this time higher than the castle walls,
higher than the big square houses, higher than the church tower,

which would toll its last from under the waters of wrath, suddenly through impending gloom broke the perfect arched magic of the Bow of Reconciliation. And my father, with his gay irrelevance, would point out the primary colours hovering above the 'Ivy Bush' and mystify us by remarking that, if they could be mixed together, they would produce the purest of whites, purer than Chinese white, whiter than the matchless white he himself could make by adding a touch of blue. And indeed the colours did look divinely pure and fresh—transparently unreal—above the shining slates and dripping chimney-pots.

As Scripture had promised, the sun shone once more on the just and the unjust—if only for an hour. Cautiously, with strong boots and gloves on, carrying wraps and umbrellas, we would be taken for a walk to the Parade or to that part of it which the people who lived there called the Esplanade.

Out of a deep blue sky in which turriform masses of silvery whiteness were sailing at ease, a dazzling suffusion of light would fill the air and be reflected from the prismatic emerald of the drenched meadows. The little round hills almost skipped as the Psalmist had predicted; though actually, as my mind was literal from birth, it was not the hills that skipped but the small white lambs on their sides. And white as snows lodged among the brilliant greens, farms and cottages shone forth from the slopes, blinding the eyes with their white-limed walls, roofs and chimneys. That isolated cube westward was Penygraig Chapel from which you could catch, above the gleam of the bay, the keep of Llanstephan. Here was Danyrallt, where a gentleman called Steel, to whom my father fondly referred as Dick, had come from London to sojourn off and on, to drink a great deal and one day to wed. The large farm that had replaced the mansion he used to visit seemed to us none the worse for the recent deluge. Right above it rose Llangunnor, concealing on another slope its small church and black yew trees high against the sky. On its flanks, we were vaguely told, was buried Merlin the Enchanter. That was Merlin's hill, across the horseshoe bend of the stream, that shapely hill, distinct from the line of bare heights, with its crown of larches. How fine it would be to take train to Abergwili at its foot, then climb to its top and look down on Grongar, about which someone called Dyer had made verses, which someone else, also a poet, but very important, had deigned to praise. And beyond the

ruins of Dryslwyn, rising steep from the bed of the river, on the opposite bank was Golden Grove, where in troublesome times a man of meditation had retired to write *Holy Living* and *Holy Dying*. And far beyond Golden Grove you could look straight up the valley to the great black range with Carreg Cennen at its foot—mountains at last, but so impossibly far away!

Where could one find a gentler world than this, spread at one's feet and threaded by the winding river, with now a mansion near its banks, now a ruined keep—Dryslwyn and Dynefor, Green Castle and Carreg Cennen? Where indeed, and by what queer fate was I doomed to remain unresponsive for so long to its sequestered classic loveliness? What disruptive complex of discontent and deep romantic yearning for other sights, other ways, other climes was to expatriate me for half a lifetime from its charm and benediction? Was it the rains alone that washed this joy away, or some distemper of blood and nerves clamouring to be healed by prospects alien, grandiose, abysmal—by anything but the refined solicitude of the mild domestic scene?

THE OLD HOUSE

Most of our home life was spent in the upper storeys of a small house that juts out conspicuously into the narrow, busy main street where, before the middle of the nineteenth century, my grandfather had established himself as house painter and decorator. An air of unaltered antiquity hangs about the premises which are now scheduled as a period piece. Except for an extension which my father got built on to the back of the living room, the interiors, we felt, were dark but not gloomy. All of glass and wood the annexe shone like a bright utensil among old scullery ware. The other rooms had something of the character of those engraved in a popular edition of Dickens we were allowed to finger now and then. Actually there was a touch of the curiosity shop about our establishment, though we should not have thought of making a comparison so much like a caricature.

Diminutive in size but manifold in character, the old house as I knew it was honeycombed with variously appointed haunts. By the time you had descended from a bedroom on the top floor, had looked in at the kitchen or glanced at the street through a front

window and then plunged into the darkness that led by a flight of easy wooden stairs down to the shop; when you had sidled along the crates that lined the passage with sheets of glass packed in straw and, crossing the yard, had looked in at the workshop to survey the paints or had turned aside to climb the steps to the "top shop"— a dusty lumber-room over a long-suffering bakery—half-an-hour might have slipped away without much to show for the zigzags and gradients of the journey.

You still cannot miss 15 King Street. Its frontage advances a yard or more beyond the other houses and extends for about twenty-five feet along the narrow pavement. It is flanked by higher buildings in one of which an old woman and her two daughters used to sell the bread they baked. The other, the "Probate", is the quietest office on earth. Very high and strongly built of rusticated ashlar protected (in my youth) by iron railings, it remains the lofty image of discreet bureaucracy, but it is an adolescent of 1875 compared with the humble dwelling it protects from the sou'-westers. Recent refurbishings on the façade of a house opposite disclosed the date 1720. My impression is that the one I was born in was built at least a little earlier. Its frontage received but one significant alteration when my grandfather took over in the Victorian forties.

Near the bed I slept in when a child hung a couple of reproductions in sepia, carefully framed. The objects attracted no definite attention, or perhaps they repelled inspection. A flicker of the candle might catch one of them, projecting into my dreams a drama of obscurely tragic significance. It probably represented angels descending into the glooms and fires of a vast arena to bear aloft the souls of Christian martyrs. But I seem never to have had the curiosity or the courage to stand up in bed and face the thing out.

What I dreaded most was that for one reason or another my mother should miss coming upstairs to sing me to sleep. With her is associated the deepest of all affections, but she was not demonstrative or expansive. An Englishwoman bred of a stock that was, if anything, Anglican, she was particularly reserved about religion. Why does she sing that strange, ingratiating, disturbing hymn:—

> Joyful, joyful, will that meeting be!

The words had a curious ring. An embryonic sense of contradiction was suggested by them long before I could grasp what a contradiction

meant. That meeting is not the same kind as meeting my mother here, or the rest of the family downstairs, or any meeting in town or in chapel or anywhere in this world. "In a moment, in the twinkling of an eye, at the last trump . . ." It is something like that. What does mother make of it all, quietly singing there? To ask her outright is impossible. People brush such questions aside. Besides they are very hard to find words for. "Joyful, joyful . . .?" But the tune has changed. "Sicilian Mariners" has come round. This is much nicer. The black gondolas swing gently on the tide, then move off silently into the deep.

Sleep has come and gone and tomorrow is struggling through the small shut panes, with their blinds and thick curtains. Draughts my father, the healthiest of men, cannot endure; he scorns this modern fad about air indoors. Here he is like a bird waiting for breakfast, his small hands ready to hop among the cutlery and, to my mother's annoyance, skilfully balancing knives, forks and spoons till the meal is ready. Like a bird he eats just crumbs of everything with gusto and discouraging rapidity.

How sane and familiar everything seems by daylight! One is tired of it all by noon. One could easily sleep after dinner to the strains of a German band from a distant street corner. After tea the shadows return more or less quickly. It is soon time for bed. One is sleepy, of course, but now that it is quite dark the uncontrollable wish is there not to be left alone with—I cannot think what. Nothing "untoward" had happened or was ever to happen while we were young. Sickness was often in the home. Sometimes it was a serious affliction, but sooner or later it passed. We realised what death meant, but it was never a reality to us in our childhood. Our elders were patient, sensible and balanced. And when we descended to the level of the street, there was my father, perhaps in a laughing mood, ready to grant any moderate request; or in a fury to be shunned at full speed before he had time to snatch up a roll of wallpaper and play kettle-drum on our retreating quarters as we scamper upstairs. And whatever the paternal mood, from the background of the "office" or from the desk by the window in the shop, a genial grave face would smile down on us, the discords and harmonies of the years making not a whit of difference to Uncle Robert's even temper.

CHAPTER THREE

LEARNING TO READ

A S a reader I was certainly no prodigy. Compared with my visual and plastic initiations reading seems to have played a minor role in my early education. Our volume of *Chatterbox* with its tarnished covers and black and white woodcuts must have been old-fashioned before our time. It was never a favourite, and I doubt if any of its contents were read through. They seemed gloomy, moralizing and unexciting, the sort of good literature for which I had an instinctive apathy. The Bible could be ignored since we heard it read five times a Sunday. Another collection, called after its binding the Red and Blue book, was better liked. It had coloured illustrations which seemed more up to date. I don't remember any of its stories, but some of them may have been read, as it was a daily companion. Its real attraction was the abundance of pictures which could be copied in pencil and paint.

Of earliest reactions to reading all I can now recall is that I had some taste for adventure, hardly any for sentiment (usually less amorous than lacrimose), and none for gratuitous tragedy. Characteristic, I'm afraid, was my antipathy to fantasy. Fantasy was not gripping; it wasn't real. A tardy perception of the beauty and value of this quality has made me wonder whether extraneous forms of it are not too often forced upon a child's attention before his imagination is supple enough to accept them, or when he is preoccupied, so to speak, with the fantasy of the real things he is discovering around. I was not pestered with much fantastic literature, but my early reactions to certain imaginative works may be worth trying to describe.

Pilgrim's Progress repelled me with what seemed its combination of unreality and moralizing. My mother, the daughter of a northern farmer, scoffed at episodes in the tale; but I was not put off it at second hand. The allegory itself was too obvious to convince one that actual facts were being recorded, and then why put up with more religious instruction when reading for pleasure? Sunday was full of that sort of thing. Nor could the *Arabian Nights* hold me for long.

There was something equally disquieting, curious, queer about such oriental stories as we found in abridged forms in our penny weeklies, Aladdin, Sinbad and everything Chinese. They were all a little sinister.

Hans Andersen's fairy tales were much preferred to Grimm's. The latter had such sad endings which threatened from the start. Not that a tale had to end happily to be acceptable. Mystery was never unpalatable; but unrelieved tragedy, however much heroism or virtue it evoked, made me impatient. Nor should morbidity be pushed too far. That was the unfortunate effect produced by *Alice in Wonderland*. To drop through a hole in the earth and swim about in a lake of your own tears with a mouse and other animals as big as yourself—that wasn't very nice, was it? And as for going through a looking glass, that meant burying yourself alive in an old brick wall. The feel of that crumbling aridity remains with me to this day. Although I have found a taste for Wonderland, the courage has never come to go further than the title of *Alice through the Looking Glass*.

It was romance that attracted me. By romance I mean not modern sentiment, but, to begin with, those alluring imitations which copious hacks and plagiarists drew off and diluted from the pure springs of Abbotsford and the Border. I must have been quite young when something occurred which I must try to recall in detail as I rank this and its sequel as one of the very rare literary revelations of my boyhood. Rudimentary as it was, nothing throughout my early schooling could compare with it as an initiation to a certain kind of literary interest and feeling.

In the small bedroom under the roof of the old house the two children are awakened as usual by their father rushing in to rouse them with the first news of the day: eight o'clock and pouring with rain.

"Much too early", they shout. "Tell us a story instead". The little man jumps in beside them and plunges into some tale of chivalry or legend, never quite authentic nor told in the grand manner. The story leaps from point to point; action dominates the scene; no-one has time for love-making or bemoaning fate. The thick leaves on the wallpaper seem to stir as if an arrow had shot through them. More arrows fly past. Parting the boughs and dashing down the glade there go Robin Hood and his merry men, dressed in

Lincoln green with red lapels and eagles' feathers stuck in their caps. Swiftly they move across the sward, off in pursuit of that proud old Abbot riding along the edge of the forest with his train of serving men and bags of gold he shouldn't have.

Events move faster than in a modern film. The story flits from deed to deed, confusing the small boy with its lack of logic: 'But why did he do that next?' 'Why? Goodness knows: that's how it was.' By now the forest has opened and a high keep appears on the skyline. The portcullis is up, the drawbridge down, and there's a dungeon underneath. It looks as if a tournament is going on under the ramparts. Tournament? It's a fight to the death.

The two knights are prancing, tilting, withdrawing, charging, vizors down, at each other with their long lances fixed, or hacking and hewing with their swords. Look out! there's one lance splintered. It's the small knight's and he's the good one. The big bad one, hated and feared by everybody, is terrifically strong: he has never met his match so far. But watch the little fellow now: he's riding rings round him. There! he's in with his sword. Round and round they whirl. He's in again. The big chap can't use his lance now. He's just a second too slow in changing weapons. The small knight's up in his stirrups and with a tremendous stroke splits the monster, armour and all, *cap-à-pie*!

With that mighty stroke my father brings his right arm down on the quilt and, using its leverage, jumps out of bed. With a whirl of white calico and a call over his shoulder to get up at once, he flings out of the room and plunges into the bath he had contrived to perch on the dark landing at the top of the stairs. A few cold splashes and much rubbing and blowing, and he is ready for breakfast. And so, more or less, are the rest of us.

The experiment must often have been repeated. But many of my father's other stories have faded out of recollection, leaving a vague afterglow like that shimmer on the snowy Vans I have tried to describe. One of them indeed seems to revert magnetically to the borderland of consciousness where memories become inchoate, yet remain vaguely tenacious. This was not a tale of action or warfare; it left an impression of benign generosity, primitive yet civilized, with a hint of something sacred yet infinitely human, told briefly without a touch of unction.

Figures appear, far away in time and place. They stand expectantly

on rising ground surrounded by immense fields of golden corn. The figures wear turbans and their flowing robes show up in different colours against the yellow depths of the harvest. The centre of the group is an old man, hale, venerable, and of a most genial dignity. The elder and his kinsman are looking with great joy towards someone who is approaching through the corn, a young man not yet in the picture, but whom they have come to greet. Is he the Prodigal Son? Or has the prodigal become confused with Joseph, and the roles of Joseph and his brethren been reversed through the imprecisions of memory? The identity of the figures in this faded narrative puzzles me still; so does the way it was told. How could my father's abrupt sketchiness have produced the impression I retain of immortal welcome? For the old man is not God. My father wasn't preaching or teaching; nor was he making up a tale for the kiddies. He was drawing no doubt on Old Testament sources; but he was not contaminating them as I am doing now over sixty years later, when the great myths have fallen into disuse. Perhaps his fondness for pictures had suggested a touch of colour or a gesture here and there. Or, what is more likely, the pictorial touches may have come in from some old lithograph or coloured plate disturbed in a corner-cupboard when I was rummaging for something new to read.

Abraham and Isaac was another tale he told; but this left a clear impression. The boy would argue and his father would dodge the issue, but he kept to the theme. 'Abraham, you see, is collecting sticks for the sacrifice of his small son.' 'Why of his small son?' 'God ordered it just to see if Abraham would obey. And he hadn't gathered many sticks when an angel appears and says: "It's all right, Abraham, you've got the sticks together; you needn't light up: God's satisfied." ' 'But what was Isaac doing all the time? Couldn't he have heard?' 'Isaac? Oh Isaac was playing with the goat and kicking up no end of a shindy.'

My Sunday school-teachers were earnest men but, lacking such gifts as these, they left no image on the mind. The most powerful image, I can't help thinking, was a favourite with my uncle as well as my father: Exodus. How often have I heard it emerge in my uncle's extempore prayers! My father, talking to the children, would relate the great story in language as simple as scripture, though not in memorized biblical diction.

Quickly the scene unwinds. A dark crowd, a company you couldn't number, advances along the shore of the Red Sea. But it is not the breakaway from Egypt, nor the waves of the sea (as it might be between Ferryside and Llanstephan) held back at full tide like two walls of water, nor through the gap the figure of Moses found among the bullrushes, nor the great leader himself led by the pillar of fire at night and the pillar of cloud by day: all this is quickly subsumed in the hasty words of the storyteller. What remains?

The scene has become still, just as my father could sketch it with a stump of soft pencil and a rub of the thumb. Above the sea the moon is fixed in a sky of livid heat. The tide has ebbed and on the gleaming sands appear dark masses left high and dry as the slow waters recede. What are these dark masses? Not reefs covered with sea-weed as at Tenby . . .   Next Sunday the great hymn rings out:

. . . 'and Phaoroh's warriors strew the shore.'

Between this and the next event in my reading a gap of a few years was bridged by those useful pink paperbacks called *Books for the Bairns*. Apart from the Bible what little I knew of mythology came first through them. For some reason that still puzzles me neither the classical nor the Chinese fables could hold my attention. The former seem to have struck me as conventional, though how I formed this opinion is hard to tell, unless it came from comparisons with the Biblical fables and records which were presented us as real. As for the Chinese stories there was as I have said, something sinister about them and the feeble drawings that accompanied the letterpress, which created antipathy for years. It lasted, I fear to think, up to the revelation of Chinese art which astonished me in the Academy exhibition. This delay in recognition illustrates the mischief of giving children poor texts to read in their most impressionable years and especially cheap illustrations which, in a sense, may fix their sight for ever, and blind them prematurely to the beauties of the originals. I can even now recall the relief I felt when the pink series of classical 'superstitions' yielded to the tales of Brer Rabbit. The thrills these gave were, I admit, of a fantastic order, but the fantasy derived from natural themes.

I would be still a youth when my father handed me a cheap paper back with an illustrated cover, which he had picked up at a news-agent's on the way home. It was one of a popular series re-hashing

episodes from Scott. This introduction was another of the few great discoveries of my boyhood; the thrill of it is with me now. The light filtering through the glades of Sherwood and reflected in those double columns of close print provided magic enough for me. The exploits of the men in Lincoln green had sufficient probability to hold my interest and stock my dreams. Besides, Sherwood forest was still alive, full of the oldest oaks, and it stood somewhere within the magic circle surrounding my mother's home . . .

These small books absorbed my weekly pence until the quality of the series degenerated. My father spotted this quickly and advised my dropping the subscription. I resisted for a time. But soon it was clear that the tales which had been the most refreshing and exhilarating I had ever read were becoming more and more extravagant variations on their predecessors. The tone of the penny horrible had crept in, and that was never an allurement. One frightening scene in which a captive had been kept so long in a dungeon that he would rush like a frantic animal at the daily gobbets of food thrown down, finished me off. It has often recurred to me when I think of Auschwitz.

It was now that my father conferred the greatest boon of my youth. I was ready, he thought (though with some hesitation), for *Ivanhoe* and those other favourites of his, *Quentin Durward* and *The Fair Maid of Perth*. I recall the feeling of transition from one level of style to a higher, from an easy to a more stately tempo, from a *Boy's Own* story to a novel for grown-ups. Gradually the new charm worked, and the stoutly bound volumes of Scott's tales, carefully preserved in the small bookcase behind the office door, yielded to my wrapt progress with this branch of English literature. From a child I have been much too self-conscious to forget what I was doing when awake. But this was not like reading, but like living through vast imaginative experiences that were exciting but true. For years I felt it an affront to criticize Scott's style and as for his 'long-windedness', this seemed to me a masterly contrivance of deferment which sustained the interest by suspending the narrative. The reader, however, must not be deceived by this apparent absorption in the Waverley Novels. My enthusiasm was based on acquaintance with only a few of them—those that are now considered the least good.

Woodstock defeated my ardour. Dickens came next with *David Copperfield* and *A Tale of Two Cities*. These I preferred to *Oliver*

Twist, which my father recommended as a masterpiece. For *Pickwick*, one of his greatest favourites, I was not old enough. *Westward Ho!* resumed in one last pitch of excitement my fervour for romance, before examination syllabuses undertook to prescribe my reading and to apply it to purposes incompatible with the enjoyment of the book in hand. More and more of my time was to be spent 'studying'. But rarely again in early life were books to be memorable events. Not even in my childhood could they keep me long from what was to be seen or heard indoors or out.

*

* *

Thanks to the stability of the times, a man with four or five children, working partner in a small business, could in my youth go through life without a serious financial care or at least without admitting any he may have had, save to his wife. My father is not perhaps a test case, as a less mercenary-minded man could scarcely be found. Money he never mentioned except to say he hadn't any. Nor can I recall having seen him handling cash except when arranging copper and silver coins poured out of a small crimson velvet bag in which, as sidesman, he had collected the Sunday's offerings.

The older I get the more I realize how much of what I value in education came to me directly or indirectly from him. Yet he was not a teacher in the pedagogical sense. What he did for me in his off-hand way I cannot help differentiating from anything like the methods and results of systematic education. My earliest initiation to good reading was entirely due to my father's hints and tips, and by good reading I mean the reading of good books with attention and *with enjoyment*. Nothing of this kind was acquired through my early schooling. This omission is one of the few big flaws of which I am still conscious in the curriculum and the instruction at the elementary grade. Where, apart from their own reading, people of my father's type and period got their literary education from, puzzles me, unless it came mainly from hearing the Bible read and discussed in their chapels and Sunday Schools. Not that my father could be called a Bible reader. Most people of his class and generation were familiar with the best passages of Scripture and had

its images and rhythms inscribed in their blood. What knowledge he had of Shakespeare's plays I am not inclined to underestimate, even though the close-printed copy in the Lansdown series was our sole household collection. My attention was drawn to some of their familiar passages simply by hearing them recited in the course of whatever job was in hand. This is more than can be said for the gabble indulged in by way of presenting the tragedies and comedies prescribed in university courses. My father's favourite reading was, of course, modern and the best of it had been done before my time. Complaints used to be made because, when left in charge of the shop, 'Arny' would so often be found buried in a book in the office. The chief English novels of the 18th and 19th centuries he was familiar with as well as with those by the great continental and American writers which everyone was supposed to have read, Hugo, Dumas, Tolstoy, Dostoievsky, Fenimore Cooper, Mark Twain and Washington Irvine. Of the vanity of the autodidact my father hadn't a trace. He would frequently point out the big readers of the town as they passed up and down King Street. One of these was a tall intelligent man who was twice Mayor and who may still be remembered as Henry Howells, the photographer, with whose wide literary culture my father would contrast the limits of his own. What so often he did for me was to distinguish in a phrase the author, the title, and something to the point about the interest or the character of a book: off I would go to the Institute library in the Assembly rooms, or to the small one he helped to run in the Sunday Schoolroom, to borrow and sample the volume with which I was rarely disappointed. Recommendations at the university level were always to reference books, never to masterpieces. My teachers were modest; this word 'masterpiece' they didn't and couldn't honestly use much.

Considering his upbringing and environment my father was decidedly broadminded. The toleration he extended to some men and ideas at first puzzled a son for whom names like Tom Paine and Robert Blatchford had faintly suspicious implications. *Frondeur* is the word I like to use of him in a critical mood. He was slightly, perhaps subtly, subversive in his judgments, always ready to laugh at Victorian pretensions and proprieties and to treat snobbery as a joke. In poetry his taste was, within narrow limits, similar to that of Lord Wavell, his preferences being for narrative

poems inspired by chivalry or romance like Scott's, or lyrics of action like Byron's, or again the old English ballads, from one of which, 'Sir Percy Spens,' he selected my name. My love of Wordsworth came not from my father, but (I like to think) from instinctive rather than literary impulses on my mother's side and her father's love of the land. Tennyson was the last in date of the poets who found favour at home. A thick green volume of his works was part of the household stock of books: it had been sufficiently used to become detached at the seams. As for Browning, it is not easy to guess how many of his poems were read by my elders. Most literate persons seem to have thought it fashionable to refer to him. But the difficulties encountered in *Sordello* and *The Ring and the Book* were notorious, and were frequently cited as obstacles to progress beyond the few favourites.

Once in later life a lady whose house was one of those he often visited on business errands asked my father what *other* poet's work he would accept as a gift. He and I reviewed our joint resources and I suggested the poems of Coleridge. And so I am able to read 'Frost at Midnight' in the small volume given to him by Mrs. Edward Morris of Brynmyrddin. Fond as he was of reciting a line or a phrase of great verse for the fun of the thing, my father's verbal memory, though better than my own, was not good enough to tempt him to bore whatever company he was in with long quotations. His manner was always light and at times satirical or comic. From him one picked up cues of value, less like those of a dominie than those of a discreet prompter for whom the play's the thing. How far away one was from that popular type of examination question, "Identify *ten* of the following passages" . . .

When on rare occasions he indulged in a judgment, conventional as it might sound, it was accompanied by the feeling of a man who had read for himself and believed in the view he was passing on. Once in his quick way he referred to Wolfe reciting lines from Gray's *Elegy* as he went up the St. Lawrence to take the Heights of Abraham and lose his life. 'That', he said, 'and *The Burial of Sir John Moore* are considered the best short poems in the English language.'

From all my memories of him one gesture stands out with a gleam as bright as the brilliant night on which it happened. I was at home working in a backroom and in a stew of anxiety over some

confusing problem involved in preparing for an examination. The glass door was open on to the garden behind the house. From it a cheerful voice broke in with a tentative mixture of appeal and apology: 'Come out a minute and look at the sky!'

It was one of those limpid nights when, in our rain-washed atmosphere, whole systems of visible luminaries hang low in the sky, each seeming to outblaze the other as they rush away from us. Stars, however bright and near, were as distant as anything in heaven or earth could be from the clotted muddle my work was in. Grudgingly, and merely to respond to the call, out I go, to hear my father read off the constellations with a direct ease I couldn't emulate even now. An immense breath of freshness invaded my lungs and brain. Light in darkness! Serenity! Order! The contrast between my state of desperation, caught in the fuddled compulsions of the time, and the freedom of my father's fancy, roving but not lost among the luminous expanses above, has never left me.

Chapter Four

ROMANTIC EDUCATION

THE period from the end of my primary schooling up to and including my first two years at the University was in many ways the worst I have survived. It could be a desperately hard time for any young aspirant to learning. But what clouds darkened my path sooner or later showed silver linings, and most of my grammar school experience must be excepted from this gloomy verdict. Nor should I forget to recall that human aspects were always favourable. Good parental relationships and consistently loyal, ever increasing friendships have been the sustaining boons of my life. Its unfavourable aspects (how often have I told myself) seemed to come obscurely from within and to erupt mainly in bouts of ill-health which could at times check progress and turn it into an obstacle race.

The way to higher things lay through that stiff but almost universally valid test, the London Matriculation. But to matriculate I should have to go to the grammar school of the town, and home finances couldn't rise to that. The County of Carmarthen, the largest in Wales, was not famous for generosity in the encouragement of educational aspirants. It offered only one scholarship capable of providing enough to cover fees and other costs. The rare boys from the town who had won this distinction were regarded as pupils of exceptional ability. I was not of their calibre and I knew it. Although generally successful in tests, I was not a reliable examinee and, with plenty of will to work and lively interests, I could never quite feel I had a sufficiently clear, retentive type of mind to ensure a top place.

At this juncture there occurred the first of many useful coincidences or vital strokes of luck that have carried me and my baggage of woes and aspirations on to the next stage of the climb. The local education authority had decided that part of the training for pupil-teachership should henceforth be provided at a centre created in the grammar school of the town. It was thus that my companions and I got in, if not by the front portal, at least by a side door opening

on a world of interests, ancient and modern, that were new to us and often, if not always, exhilarating.

*

*   *

The leisurely but serious régime of Queen Elizabeth's Grammar School must have received a shock at having to accommodate a group of senior youths bred in an alien tradition and thrust upon the attentions of a staff whose signed commitments to the ancient institution did not include servicing a preparatory training centre for pupil teachers. The centre on the other hand would have been a mediocre affair but for its casual contact with the school. The nucleus of our preparation was a separate responsibility of the English master, who became in a sense our director of studies. This rough set-up was hardly a success. The group of novices to whom I belonged would have benefited from more specific attention and above all from stronger discipline. Liberated from teaching commitments for three days a week, we were inclined to take things easy and to greet the 'higher learning' with humorous disrespect. Catcalls could interrupt work in class and guffaws follow solemn interdictions. Parts of the instruction were feeble enough to excuse the lads for kicking their heels rather than 'taking it down'. But serious teaching, when it occurred, could evoke serious response.

The official objective of the course was to prepare us for the Preliminary Certificate of the Board of Education. This examination we took after two or three years' work and most of us passed in the tests. For reasons that will appear later I sat the examination twice, gaining a couple of distinctions on the first occasion and three or four at the second shot. Several of my companions in this course became successful teachers ultimately, and some retired as respected headmasters.

At the Grammar School I made acquaintance with a number of fresh subjects: Latin, for instance, and Chemistry, both of which were well taught. A new world was opened by the latter, giving a meaning and an interpretation to physical nature around one, hitherto completely unsuspected. I can recall the sensation of the sudden dawning intelligibility of things that came with those first chemical equations, the composition and decomposing of simple

substances giving the clue to the structure of the universe; so that in principle we captured the nebulae and fabricated stars in our test-tubes and crucibles. I am still nonplussed by the truth that soap is a salt. But who could disbelieve Mr. Coles, one of the best teachers I ever had? It will be thought an exaggeration but I affirm that, unlike almost any other teacher I heard at this or a later stage, Mr. Coles gave the impression of thoroughly knowing his job, by which I mean that he knew his subject so as to be able to teach it not only efficiently, but effectively. Never fervently, of course (Mr. Coles came from the Cavendish), but with a clear, reasonable fascination.

Mr. Firth, a wrangler, was 'more of a genius', but not so clear a teacher. It may be simply that he tried to teach us 'maths.', a subject for which I had no enthusiasm. I remember his fury because we Pentrepoeth boys preferred our slick formulas to his self-explanatory methods, which we thought roundabout but which actually required thought. Otherwise he shared Coles's humorous-serious attitude to work, along with an air of easy distinction and authority. They were ingratiating masters, the more so perhaps because you couldn't play the fool with them. They had that most useful and impressive quality in a teacher—tone without pomposity. Tone was the mark of the Headmaster, with a touch of emphasis variously appraised.

When I review the personalities of my teachers one stands clear in imaginative appeal from the genial but on the whole unimpressive sequence I have passed on the highroads and byways of Enlightenment. Should I be tempted to reproach the others for the amount of time we trifled away so laboriously together, all my reserves of admiration would have to be offered to the exception, although the vagaries of my harassed career allowed him little time to add to my equipment.

E. S. Allen stood at a parting of the ways on that strip of the educational landscape where my lot was cast. Having succeeded to the direction of an old English Grammar School buried in an extremity of Wales, he had for thirty years or more elegantly maintained the *ancien régime* despite changing demands and an altered spirit among the rank and file of his pupils. An admirably thorough teacher of the classics, Mr. Allen also laid the foundation of my knowledge of French, which he taught in the classical manner, but as well as any teacher of that language I was ever to have.

Had he shown more fervour for Post-Darwinian culture, none of his boys could have found reasonable grounds to demur from unanimity of approval.

But I am in no mood for reservations. Mr. Allen was the nearest approach I have known to the ideal headmaster. The traditions sat easy on his shoulders. He had the unquestionable authority that manners and breeding of themselves can give. And they could permit him to be forceful enough, when occasion demanded. As a personality, he was attractive though aloof. To say that he had charm might be a doubtful compliment, because the word, though not inapplicable, has too effeminate a connotation to be fitting for so English a type.

Allen had a fine athletic figure, tall and spare with aquiline features and a high forehead, lit by magnificent, wide grey eyes that could, it is true, blaze with the whitest fires of anger. Usually there was sincerity in their gaze with something almost like naïveté. There was naïveté, certainly, in some of his mannerisms. His jokes, in particular, were as feeble, we thought, as they were hoary. But to counterbalance these depressions there were moments of elevation in his classes, and with them I associate some of the deepest thrills of my schooldays. To be praised by Allen was a supreme reward. The voice was infinitely distinguished but natural and by no means always soft or low. I recall its accents best in connection with a summer term's work on a portion of the *Metamorphoses*. The wistful story comes back with its associations. Halcyon days! But one remembers perhaps with most gratitude the occasions when he would interrupt the lesson by taking down the plays of Shakespeare and reading a passage aloud. *That*, some of us might think in quest of a touchstone to judge the rest of our training by, was education.

With Mr. Allen the memory of a gentleman and a tradition will pass unmourned. It is nothing, perhaps, that I recall him in profile, kneeling at the small desk in the big window in an attitude of real, if not rapt, devotion; and that I still hear the prayer he is reciting in a voice that matches its beauty. To-day we look for greater efficiency, democrats for democracy, bristling doctorates from our new universities, better results, more numerous prizes. All these are good things. May we inherit them all and may they satisfy us! Let our dreams be practical, precise, productive. A tall figure in

white strolls off the playing fields. His microcosm is shattered. Why should it haunt us still?

Soon after leaving school I was obliged to return to ask the Headmaster for a testimonial in support of university entrance. He was sitting on a deck-chair in front of the school house. After inquiring about the subjects I was proposing to offer he asked, 'And what of the classics?' I hedged with the admission that further Latin would be compulsory. 'What about Greek?' he said. 'It would be a pity to miss the greatest mind of all . . .' He paused for a second. 'Plato?' came to my lips. 'Aristotle,' he said.

*

*   *

Those who have influenced us most are often those we knew least well. A longer acquaintance might have lessened their ultimate effect. This, however, would not be true of another influential figure, doubtless of far more practical and intimate importance to me, under whose spell I came while at Carmarthen Grammar School.

One day an unusual incident happened in the course of a chemistry class. A stranger wearing a gown walked into the room and began to converse with our teacher. He was a newcomer to the staff, an English master of striking, curiously romantic, appearance. He looked like a sort of mild, good Byron. Just the same arrangement of marvellous, soft brown curls; though with a primness about his high white collar that contrasted severely with the open throat of the poet's familiar portraits. Remarkably blue eyes, bright and liquid, shone pensively. The rest of the face, while it did not belie these signal features, suggested a character brimful of friendliness but with more facility than concentration or command.

Mr. Harry Thomas I still regard as one of the most potent personal influences in my early life, and in some ways as one of the most helpful. There was a vivid, succouring humanity about him. The pellucid softness of his cerulean gaze fell like balm on the toils of the flesh or the troubles of the spirit. For those who had neither toils nor troubles he lacked the severity to be masterful. But furtive generations of the sensitive few found in him a kindly local deity, sprung from the soil, almost one of ourselves.

His mind was of a simple, speculative turn, which is not the worst type for a teacher of inquiring youth to possess. Highly responsive to the purely romantic quality in literature, he wisely never attempted to define its charm. It was that 'that' which some of us felt for the first time emanating from a reaction of his as a mysterious but authentic reverberation. Literature, though, was but one of many subjects with which he concerned himself. What he saw in the others was rarely their substance or technique but almost exclusively their human implications and spiritual novelties. These he would intimate with delightful incongruity, sometimes in the classroom, more often on a doorstep, at a draughty street corner or just as the bell clanged and our paths crossed in the corridor. He certainly set my thoughts moving in most of the directions they have naturally followed since. Off mine would go in chase of his like a small kite after a big one, shooting over tree-tops, flitting between stars, losing its leader only too often quite beyond recovery in the intense inane.

Like the Headmaster, though in a way of his own, Mr. Thomas was careless of regulations and red tape. Mr. Allen would relegate 'instructions' to the waste paper basket with the indifference of a scholar disturbed by the importunities of a tax-collector. Mr. Thomas would con a syllabus as if it were a book of magic, musing over the spirit at the expense of the letter of its incantations. He had a genius for divagation. This could be bad for exposition but it happened to be good for one or two of us. At the least chance he would deflect into religious argument, and for the first time the incubus that weighed on my soul shook a little at a sympathetic touch. That day was a good one when he invited me to take tea with him in the rooms he then occupied in Pensarn. There the great loosening began, and although — characteristically — no particular problem was thrashed out to a solution, I became aware that problems like mine had not only disturbed thinkers in the past: some of them were being vividly discussed here and now. I risk irrelevance, but it must be recorded that we ate stewed apricots for tea. They have left for life the fresh taste of a viaticum.

Mr. Thomas had been caught by the New Theology, a movement centred in R. J. Campbell's ministry at the City Temple. He had heard Campbell preach and admired his liberalizing thought; and—whether the occasion quite permitted it or not—he was fond

(sometimes in the middle of a lesson) of referring to the ideas and interpretations that Campbell and others of a similar persuasion were propagating. A breath of relief from restrictive dogma was blowing through the free churches. But Wesleyan methodism was on the defensive and signs of resistance appeared in our own milieu. Much that I picked up from my English master came as good news, though not exactly as 'gospel': refreshing as it could be, it did not always bring conviction. No one before I came under Mr. Thomas's aegis seemed to understand anything of my confused, suppressed mental troubles. Yet nothing thorough or methodical characterized our fascinating bits of talk. Strict logic was no more typical of my mentor than of his pupil; but a quick sympathy was passing from one to the other which did much to ease the mind of the burdened youth.

I cannot describe the effects of this *rencontre* in more definite terms because no precision, no proof, no relevant facts emerged to clinch arguments or seal conviction of the truth of what one would have liked to believe. I clearly recall this feeling of ultimate inadequacy. (When I envisage similar problems today, the same feelings recur). My misgivings arose from the suspicion that the crudest things that worried me—notions like hell and eternal punishment—were not being removed but evaded. They were confronted with nothing more definite than Tennyson's 'larger hope', and this struck me as not much better than a cry of despair: the anxiety of a poet on behalf of the lost whom God had not only abandoned but condemned to abandonment for ever.

Yet I have no wish to deny that Mr. Thomas's tolerant, liberal and generous view of Christianity exerted a considerable, if indefinable, effect on my thoughts and feelings, easing a little the dead grip of the kind of orthodoxy my over-sensitiveness had extracted from the mild religiosity of the methodism I knew.

To Mr. Thomas I also owe the beginnings of my serious interest in poetry. To distinguish what this implies in my case from reading, I will say the beginnings of appreciation. Two things of value in my initiation I seem to owe definitely to him. I distinctly remember the occasion in class when, as he read Wordsworth's line.

Ethereal minstrel, pilgrim of the sky . . .

the first authentic thrill came to me from a lyric. It was quite

spontaneous, a kind of telepathic communication of one person's thrill to another, without anything reasoned or argumentative. This brief experience to which I seem to owe so much, has led me to think supremely important the personal attitude of a teacher to his subject, especially his *feeling* attitude, as conveyed to his class or, in that too much despised word, his enthusiasm. Alas, that my recollection of most lessons and teachers should be a record marked by its conspicuous absence. One seems to have heard too much of the dangers of fervour and impressionism in teaching. What I suspect in the presence of such criticism is that the critic may, if a teacher, be deficient, not perhaps in interest in his subject, but in the gift of making the subject vital or interesting to his hearers. There can be little doubt that the 'personal touch' is much appreciated by young people who as a rule cannot derive equal benefit from the cautious exposition of a superior scholar, and who get little or nothing from the indifference to the art of exposition which many of those who are paid to instruct them appear to affect.

The dangerous side of this feeling attitude and its weakness as criticism need scarcely be emphasized. My introduction to the study of literature had all the defects of one beginning with and based on an emotional approach to the English Romantic poets. It demanded of all literature a certain kind of thrill and it ruled out those kinds which couldn't provide this. Pope was no poet in Mr. Thomas's estimation and I agreed without having read more than a few lines. With no classics beyond a smattering of Latin and with a tempera-mental bias in favour of Romanticism, I have spent half a lifetime trying to correct the effects of this exclusive enthusiasm with its potent appeal and its narrow standards. It was difficult to believe for years that the touchstone for all true poetry does not necessarily lie in a taste for Shelley and Keats.

The Romantics had such a way of identifying themselves with realities of feeling! They made the French classics when one came to them seem utterly conventional. It did not occur to me that all types of literature and art have their conventions and that few, if any, are the *cris du cœur* of naked truth. One acquired a preference for the moderns as new as possible, provided they did not think too hard. One's cult of the vague, the imprecise, was the worship of a jealous god. Reverie, reflection, *recueillement* were permissible

attitudes; but logical thought was a low technical instrument like a gimlet or a spanner whose place was not in the temple.

Another radical notion which I trace to this stage has its importance in explaining the conception of literature with which I became imbued. Although I have long been persuaded of its fallacy, it still operates, I suspect, in my attempts to express myself and to understand the expression of others. It is connected with the 'problem of style', which has become so much less a *conscious* problem than it used to be. I must not affirm Mr. Thomas's responsibility, but under his inspiration I began to dream vaguely of style as a thing in itself. I certainly attempted to 'cultivate style' without attending sufficiently to thought or to adequate expression. I was heading for the crudest kind of fine writing, the kind that goes with sheer incompetence, with illiterateness. And I have had a struggle, perhaps not yet quite successful, to control this vulgar tendency.

Behind it no doubt lies an ethnical preference, a native bias by which my English master as well as his pupil was unconsciously motivated. Practically all forms of expression in Wales, especially the widespread arts of preaching and oratory, have a strong rhetorical cast. No nation on earth is, I imagine, more capable of 'paying itself with words', as the French say, unless we accept André Gide's verdict that it is the French themselves. There is involved in this superstition the Romantic conception of literary art. If the *affres du style* had not yet been mentioned in my hearing, the 'poetical' seemed the only sort of prose worth writing when one was engaged on anything above reporting what happened in the preparation of H_2O.

A backward glance over these experiences and impressions suggests a final reservation which may help to correct too personal an emphasis. It is obvious, I think, that the best acquisitions of my schooling were the results of influences operating independently of routine more often than through its appointed channels. Such influences may be considered a compliment to individuals or a credit to the school, but they were not an integral part of the official training given in accordance with a curriculum externally prescribed. As to the latter, what Latin I picked up was of obvious utility. The subject was well taught, but the smattering of that ancient tongue I came away with was barely equal to fulfilling the requirements of prewar matriculation, without which there could be no

prospect of a degree in Arts. The glimpses into English lyricism brought a new sensibility to birth, and this was to develop into the basis of a life interest. Two other useful acquisitions were first the relatively advanced initiation in Chemistry given us in three or four years; the value and pleasure of this I cannot over-estimate, though I never felt that any of the sciences was my line. And secondly the grounding in the French language. As with everything new, my progress here was slow and toilsome; although there was nothing disconcertingly novel in the methods that were used. The Headmaster was mainly responsible for the subject and he taught the language as he taught Latin, through translation into English and prose composition exercises. This was of course long before the days of oral tests or even of good pronunciation. I remember how startled we were to learn from him that what a Frenchman actually said for 'Cet homme' was 'Stum'!

I must try to suggest an effect which I think differentiates secondary from primary teaching, a difference I became vaguely conscious of while still at the Grammar School. After the years of ardous instruction received at the Pentrepoeth there seemed little more to learn in arithmetic except greater facility in the exercise called 'Approximations'. The name admirably characterizes the change I felt. At the elementary stage all efforts to teach and learn seemed to have been directed to attaining precise results by precise means. There was a right and a wrong, but no intermediary. This assumption of attainable exactitude tended to give the impression that every riddle in the universe could be solved with arithmetical accuracy, if not always by arithmetical means.

Much of what we learnt at the secondary stage undermined this confidence in clear issues and shook our assurance in the one and only right solution: through some of our new exercises we perceived we could do no more than approximate to the truth. Something of this was inculcated by the Headmaster's attitude and manner. When you brought a prose exercise to him for correction he would not always condemn outright a phrase which was not the best rendering. Provided one's version was not grammatically wrong he might say: 'But how would you like to put it this way?' All pedagogues might not approve of such temporizing. But I still think of Mr. Allen's tentativeness as a model of how to present certain subjects—and they are many—which do not permit of

absolute dogmatism. I can still see the Headmaster's considerate expression as he turns to the boy standing at his desk with his exercise open: 'Don't you think this better, Jones?'

Much anxiety about a career combined with much idealization of university life to make the prospect of 'going to college' an infinitely desirable one. It was not the least of benefits conferred by my English master that he should have encouraged me persistently to think of a degree. He also applied a little effective persuasion to my mother. What qualifications I had already picked up did not include all those required for matriculation at that time. I had failed in French at the Matriculation Examination of the London University and I had failed deservedly, not through lack of diligence, but frankly through lack of proficiency. Moreover, I had as yet no qualification in Latin. As this was imperative for entrance, the prospect looked bleak. Then by an extraordinary grace on the part of the Headmaster, induced no doubt by the interventions of Mr. Thomas, an unorthodox way was opened to my persistence. It was suggested that I should join the class that was being prepared for the School Certificate. This meant stepping down to the level of the fourth form*. Without hesitation I accepted, and my only regret is that, having passed in all the subjects I offered, I was given a couple of prizes which I felt ought to have gone to some younger boy and not to the intruder. It interests me to add that one was a leather bound copy of Wordsworth's poems in which I still read with unabated elation my favourite of all poems, the unfathomable *Lines written above Tintern Abbey*.

Meanwhile I had been concentrating privately on French for another attack on the 'London Matric.', that open sesame to so many forms of advancement. Left to my own resources, I hit upon a *pis aller* of the most utilitarian kind prompted by my recent failure. Realizing that what I lacked most when faced by the tests were words and their meanings, I decided to memorize as many as possible and by the quickest means. There at hand was a collection called Spier's *French Vocabularies*. In it lists of words were arranged in groups clearly printed on good paper with, as a rule, one English word opposite a French one. This neat collection I supplemented

---

* There were other complications. I was still being financed as a candidate for the Preliminary Certificate, and it was only on condition that I took the examination a second time that I was allowed another year.

with selections from my own reading. Of this practice I made a cult and kept it up for some years, amassing a stock of terms that have been undeniably useful. Nothing will shake my belief that I thus laid foundations for a knowledge of French sufficient not only for the immediate purpose of the test which I passed, but also to be of serious help in making me a teacher of the language. The practice of learning off strings of detached words is officially condemned, and I have no wish to defend a method so irksome and laborious. It may have been useful in my case simply as a stimulus to, or substitute for, a bad verbal memory. But no quicker way has yet been disclosed to me of how to increase one's stock of words, and I still think that the majority of students' exercises, even at the Honours stage, can show embarrassing deficiencies in vocabulary.

My time at the Grammar School ended with a period of brutal collar-work, when I struggled against slow wits, insufficient schooling and bad health to gain the necessary qualifications for entrance both to a normal Training College and to a provincial University. I feel justified in looking back on this part of my schooldays with horror. I seemed to be fighting against excessive encumbrances; and indeed I was, having, with characteristic caution and earnestness, with no little ambition and with an infinite desire to get out of the rut in which I was born (leading, as far as I could see, to the local Training College and a primary teacher's career), multiplied the number of strings to my bow considerably beyond the limits of my physical resources.

A system which made so many examinations necessary at the school-leaving stage stands self-condemned. In my last year at school I sat for the Preliminary Certificate, the London Matriculation, the Senior Certificate of the Central Welsh Board and the Entrance Scholarship at Aberystwyth, and mine was far from being an exceptional case. Yet it would be unfair to blame anyone or anything more than myself for having left school without any true cultural acquisition apart from the brief initiations and routine qualifications already mentioned. In my hurried passage through the middle forms I was too much absorbed in *preparing for the next step* to acquire much of the spirit, to say nothing of the foundations, of a liberal education, even had it been possible to secure them while at a school that lacked a library.

Yet that there were definite gains made at this stage will be

evident, and personal contacts among the most precious I had known. Enough has been said of the best of them. There would be little to add about my relations to my schoolmates. These were agreeable but uneventful. Incompetence at games was a handicap in a milieu where games, rightly, counted for much. Health was deteriorating but by no means so quickly as to prevent cycling and even amateurish fumblings at tennis and cricket. Characteristically, at the latter noble game I practised a form of stalling by planting the bat before the wickets and refusing to run risks, except when the other batsman scored. This habit attracted the amused attention of senior boys who made the half-serious suggestion that I should fill a gap in the seconds by playing my unambitious role for the benefit of the rest of the team!

A more interesting reflection on my psychology at this time comes from a very different direction. In the Junior forms I found the brilliant boy who had entered the grammar school on the strength of having gained the one and only County Scholarship. He would re-appear with colours flying still higher in any sequel to this story. It was in working beside W. J. Davies that I began to learn one of the great lessons of intellectual life. With all the 'grind' I put into appointed tasks, when the tests came, invariably and easily Davies emerged top. It was not that he did not work; he worked so economically, so efficiently and so effectively that the lead was achieved without strain or trouble. He never seemed pestered or taken unprepared, and he could apply himself with equal equanimity to any kind of subject. The lesson his progress was the first, though far from being the last, to teach me was one I will call the recognition of superiorities in others—a difficult lesson for one ambitious boy to learn from another, but a lesson my own inferiorities have never allowed me to forget.

High in the Headmaster's classroom hung a shabby sepia reproduction in an oak frame. It represented an avenue of tall slender trunks capped with bunches of brown leaves and receding over a flat lawn. Why should this unlikely object, intercepted admidst anxious or pleasant preoccupations and never deliberately faced, have so firmly fastened itself on my memory as to outlive the features of most of those with whom for many terms I worked and played?

As I was long after to discover, the subject was Hobbema's

Avenue. Its action on my mind was almost entirely unconscious. I noticed none of the details that Dr. E. M. W. Tillyard mentioned in his reference to this famous picture in *The Muse Unchained*. Actually the details and the colours I now find in the original detract from, rather than add to, my first formal impression. Its persistence has convinced me of the power works of art, although indifferently presented, can exercise even on minds that are not consciously attending to them.

CHAPTER FIVE

PARNASSUS ATTAINED

BEHOLD next a bewildered, apologetic, overgrown schoolboy shuffling nervously into the College Hall at Aberystwyth on the first night of term, when its damp green walls and gothic imitations re-echo with the rumours of a curious academic reception.

Queues of restless, jostling, jesting undergraduates are drawn up in ragged lines before a circular row of harassed professors, penned in narrow desks, with whom, I perceive, they are trying, one after another, to come to terms about the session's work. From queue to queue flit liaison officers; batches secede from one queue to another. The night wears on; professorial tempers wear thin. But the queues still concentrate like battering rams upon the single-manned citadels of the desks, only at length dwindling away, as the last clients or victims are served with, or doomed to, their appropriate or compulsory courses of study. This was called the Menagerie.

On the strength of a 'prose' paper taken in the entrance examination (on the results of which I was awarded a ten pound exhibition), the Professor of French had decided that I should begin with second year's work in French language and literature. He reminded me that a science or its equivalent was compulsory in an Arts course and he assumed that, as I was not a mathematician, I should be likely to choose Logic and Philosophy. That choice, however, was debarred because one of the lecture hours in Logic or in Philosophy clashed with an hour in his subject. I must therefore accept Political Economy. But as that subject had no first year course, an 'Ordinary' in Political Economy would have to be fitted into my second year's time-table. Elation at having been allowed to start at an advanced stage in French was somewhat dashed by this unforeseen commitment, especially as my next 'choice' was abruptly circumscribed. It had to be Intermediate Latin. Regulations left no means of escape from that. They permitted a faint sense of freedom in not hindering the selection of English for my third Intermediate. Yet as English Honours (whose distant pinnacle it seemed well to keep in sight lest anything went wrong with progress

in French) required subsidiary German, my fourth subject had to be a junior course* in that language which I approached for the first time with feelings of trepidation.

Our hero's initiation into the mental life of his Alma Mater was an introduction to external requirements of curriculum, claiming precedence over personal preference, individual taste, or desire for variety and experiment. 'Schemes of study' were fixed at the outset in obedience to strict regulations; and when once the machinery got going within this framework, it was best not to interfere with the cogs. Yet at any point in his career the intellectual development of a student might be jeopardized by the operation of an artificial rule. The Arbitrary was always ready with a snare of red tape to trip up the novice who might be tempted to follow his bent rather than be prepared to submit to the *bend* which the system was, by its nature, blindly—and not, be it noted, with deliberate intention on the part of its personnel—compelled to impose.

I remember the confusion (engaging enough to watch for those not involved) created by a disclosure, made at mid-session by the Dean of Arts, to the effect that he had unwittingly misinterpreted an obscure regulation and had misled a number of students into following a course which they must now abandon for another at all speed and cost!

Looking back I see the procedure as a kind of puppet show in which the shifting of the scenes was of far greater importance even than the mechanical gestures and gambols of the marionettes, who were worked by some indiscernible *deux ex machina* not to be identified with the Administrative or with the Teaching staff of the establishment, or even with its Principal, all of whom were jerked, bustled or thwarted by the same inscrutable, wiry will.

To save my image from the fate of an overdrawn caricature, let me hasten to add that we puppet-students a-dance with our teachers in obedience to a programme bristling with restrictions, were only occasionally conscious of the subtle limitations of our lot. We were for the most part immature with no clear intellectual will or velleity of our own. Limiting conditions are by no means always felt as disadvantages by young minds at this stage. The notion that youth

---

* That is a pre-Intermediate course of one year which did not count towards the degree total—a reasonable requirement to expect of beginners in the language.

is always free, liberal, adventurous is a romantic fallacy. The adolescent can be, and in most directions often is, stubbornly conservative while he remains adolescent. It is age that brings the philosophic mind, the open and balanced outlook—to a few favoured individuals. And at all stages, when there is plenty for the body to do, or when the mind is satisfied that it is doing its best in definite and unalterable conditions, it may be possible to enjoy a very real, if perhaps a somewhat supine, form of contentment in following a routine. Anyhow, this account would lose what value it may possess, if I pretended that my generation arrived at college, breathlessly in quest of culture. That would be absurd. But is it equally absurd to claim that a university should do something to stimulate so vague yet so valuable an ideal, or to give it some sort of substance or foundation? Schemes of study composed of mosaics of single-year courses; schemes of study, their inception and completion within fixed periods of alarming brevity, these were the Alma Mater's first bounty to her hopeful sons and daughters.

After these initial steps Jones loses sight of himself almost completely in a maze of featureless routine. Nothing stands out. The blurred retrospect of those early undergraduate years appears to have been enlivened by no memorable thrill of intellectual discovery or development.* He was certainly acquiring a number of new skills and making much needed progress with others already begun. But no opening breadth of view, no fresh wind of doctrine made him aware that he had left the schoolroom for the academic grove. A change of metaphor may suggest what really was happening. The Robot-God of the machine was playing 'pyramids' with him according to the following rules.

In my time a minimum of nine courses was required to complete a degree in arts, the Honours course, if such were taken, counting as two. These courses had to be chosen so as to represent a minimum of five different subjects. A normal arrangement for a Pass degree in Arts to be attained in three years would approximate to the following pattern: four Intermediates in the first year, three Ordinaries in the second year and two Specials in the third. An

---

* Compare the experience of Henry Adams: 'Four years of Harvard College, if successful, resulted in an autobiographical blank, a mind on which only a water-mark had been stamped.' (*The Education Act of Henry Adams: An Autobiography*, Boston and New York 1918, p. 55).

Honours degree could be attained in the same time on the following basis: three Intermediates and one Ordinary in the first year, two Ordinaries and one Special in the second, and one Honours in the third year. Other combinations and arrangements could be made within definite limits, and more courses and subjects could be taken than the nucleus here represented. But these were average requirements. Regularly fulfilled, they formed a pyramid. If Honours was aimed at, its apex must be reached not later than the fifth session.

Each year's course was not completed without a pass in an examination set by the university at the end of the session. At the end of each term the college authorities set a test in every subject at every stage. This was considered important and results were published. An undergraduate was thus examined no fewer than three times a session in every subject he was taking. Multiply this by the number of subjects taken and it will be seen that a student might have to submit to twelve, and even to more tests and examinations in a session—that is actually in about six months, between the end of the first and of the third term. No course involved less than three lecture hours a week. A register was kept of attendances in which a student had to give satisfaction in order to be 'signed up' for presentation at the sessional examination. A total of from twelve to fifteen hours of compulsory classes was an average, and twenty would be a frequent demand upon the student's time.

Measured by any conceivable standard of education other than academical, the disadvantages of such a system are obvious and in a high degree serious. That a public academy must adopt a more or less definite method in carrying out a more or less definite programme of work is a fact which I readily accept. A university is not a boundless veldt where young seekers after learning may go browsing or frolicking at will. But neither is it a narrow pen where shepherds watch their flocks with such impersonal caution as to suggest that they are less concerned with giving their sheep good pasture than with training them to keep a future wolf from the door. Thanks to the régime's effect upon teaching, such instruction as a student received in my time was forced to approximate to what is called 'spoon-feeding.' The student was not taught or (it would seem) expected to think but to memorize, and as at least fifty per cent of the teaching took the form of dictation, the examinee was often reproducing a more or less garbled version of what he had received

in class. The exigencies of the various courses discouraged him from reading widely for himself. To say that we were unable to take interest in parts of the texts prescribed would of course be untrue. But so far as I know, little *serious* reading was done beyond that strictly required by the courses. The result was a definite tendency to regard the intellectual side as uningratiating drudgery. All reference to it outside the classroom was 'talking shop', and this was ignoble. A complete divergence reigned between 'shop' and 'life'. The latter covered sport, societies, the social life in lodgings and the genial institution of the covered quadrangle where, between the classes, men and women were permitted to perambulate and mingle. This side was alive and stimulating. The intellectual side was also alive, but as a machine is alive. It was a mechanical routine working at high pressure to produce a marketable product.

Few young men and women but would have responded to a more liberal form of instruction, had there been time for it. But we must 'cover the course'. Some of our teachers would doubtless have been happy to give instruction of this kind. They too must cover the course. Otherwise we, their pupils, would be the first to complain. The practices of teacher and student were therefore rigidly *ad hoc*. The art of lecturing was reduced to translating and correcting in languages, and to the dictation of notes in most other Arts subjects. A unique opportunity for young people to hear competent men of mature grasp and good delivery discuss a topic in a broad, free, personal manner was sacrificed to the Time Machine. And one of the best intellectual advantages which a university should have to offer—the finest perhaps of all with the possible exception of direct contact with a distinguished and expert tutor—was almost totally denied.*

In such conditions as these the intrinsic urge is driven out of study. Study becomes a means, never an end. Dominated by an external objective, it is adjusted to practical purposes which are attained without friction and without fervour. And so the essential occupation of the student becomes perfunctory and degraded. Those who in my time set the emphasis on work alienated themselves from the moderates—often the brighter individuals—and were despised by

---

* Not quite. The year began with an Inaugural lecture which was sometimes memorable. Gilbert Murray, Sir Walter Raleigh and W. B. Yeats, who read some of his poems, were among those heard to advantage in my time.

the 'rotters', a minority who tried to paint our sober milieu in the colours of Arcadia. Regular application was common. But the man who was suspected of working hard in private could become the object of an intense irrational disapprobation. The spirit of that popular masterpiece which represented the scholar nobly absorbed, 'while other men sleep', was replaced in the standards of my student days by suspicions of the 'swot', surreptitiously stealing a march on the progress of the community, while other men played.

A second prejudice closely allied to this was characterized by an antipathy to the highbrow which amounted to a practical exclusion of the species from our midst. For this riddance one should not be ungrateful. Yet it is possible for a group to be so distrustful of 'superior' qualities that originality, distinction and those eccentricities which add grace or amusement to social culture are discouraged and suppressed. Adolescence is an inextricable mixture of delicacies, gaucheries and affectations. Stamp on excess, prohibit mannerism, and the refinements of which they are the immature excrescences may be crushed in the bud. The kind of excellence that could be proved in examinations was not uncommon among my contemporaries, but they rarely showed signs of intellectual virtuosity. Debates could be vigorous but personal discussion was feeble. Vehement contention was far more common than subtle dialectic. Humour was superabundant: irony was confused with sarcasm and detested. So we remained sanguine, uncritical juveniles, confident in our immaturity, vaguely longing for better things; with rare exceptions, incurious of the world outside, unadventurous, contented with our lot (for it was a good life), responsible, loyal, hopeful—clay waiting the potter's hand. Rarely could academic initiative have had an easier—I do not say a richer—opportunity. In readiness of response, in social bonhomie, in serenity of personal relationships knit and matured amid incomparable amenities of natural scene and atmosphere and offering foundations for a true intellectual community, our Alma Mater could claim to have effected a unique achievement. But it was an achievement in need of a finishing touch.

As in my schooldays, it was my fortune throughout my undergraduate career to meet with but one teacher who dominated, while he respected, the conditions to which his pupils had to conform. This was the Professor of Latin who took us 'freshers' in the *Epistles* of Horace. The impression these classes left on the minds of some

of us was that of a combination, unique in our experience, of good scholarship, refined taste and admirable clarity of exposition. Here for once my exacting academic dream was realized. Still fresh in mind are the signs of care with which nice or knotty points in the text were discussed, with an acuteness and authority beyond our immediate needs, the refined familiarity of diction used in construing, and the urbane seriousness of the scholar as, with tall figure bowed over the text, he strode slowly up and down the aisles of the long classroom in which a hundred of us roughly prepared lads and lasses were gathered for compulsory Latin.

My knowledge of that language was so scanty that I had to follow with excruciating attentiveness. But I still treasure my copy of the *Epistles* with every word of the oral translation written above, between or alongside the text. A vile habit; but I was facing my first Intermediate examination—and think of my schooling!

I have another memory. A terrific storm is raging around an exposed room in which a faithful remnant are attempting to take notes. A frail voice almost effaced by the din emits a remark now and then which flies or falls like a drenched bird struggling against the deluge that cataracts down the panes or gushes up through the woodwork as if determined this time to submerge our Ark of learning. The man at the wheel is desperately annotating a prescribed text. And we persist in the hope of picking up something useful for the morrow. Context questions have a way of recurring in examination papers.

On another day the door into the same classroom opens and out slips a small man who, without raising his eyes, is rapidly dictating by the time he reaches his desk. Sixty heads are already bowed; the napes of sixty necks undulate to the rhythm of sixty pens for nearly sixty minutes. So strong is the spell, so regular the drone, that one might have thought his notebook had taken the lecturer on its knee and set his chin wagging like that of a ventriloquist's doll. Nothing was gained from attending his classes except the scribble we took away. This saved us from reading the critics in print. A hired amanuensis would have served our purpose perfectly.*

Again the scene changes. A lady with a far-away look in her eyes and a taste for pursuing Icelandic sagas in and out of season waits for

* This is precisely what I heard a student say to a group of professors in the presence of a Vice-Chancellor thirty years later.

someone to finish rendering a passage of Anglo-Saxon prose. The translator has got stuck like a carthorse tugging a load of stones through a bog. The lady turns to a newcomer, looking up his name in her register: 'Will you go on, Mr. Quayle?' A Cumberland voice, to the amazement and envy of the rest of us, reads off the passage as if it were a paragraph of daily news. 'Thank you,' says the lecturer for the first time in memory.

Such is my earliest recollection of my good friend, Thomas Quayle, soon the life and soul of the College, which he left a few years later with a couple of Honours qualifications and a London D.Litt. to take up the Nobel fellowship at Liverpool.

However defective the schools from which most of us had come, my companions and I often felt the loss of former guidance and personal advice. Ideally this should have forced our development. But most of us were too immature not to be embarrassed by the relative impersonality of the new mode. If the majority succeeded in steering a clear course, some of the more promising drifted into shallows without a warning before their results.

My first glance at a Prospectus had filled me with discomfort. When I became accustomed to its archaic abstractions I found that they formulated a number of specious demands which I could not imagine myself ever being able to fulfil. This didn't deter me from setting to work or from presenting myself for examination when the session ended. In none of the tests did I satisfy myself and my relief was great to find my name on the pass lists. It increased to astonishment when I discovered that usually, out of a large class, only an insignificant number would have failed. Gradually dawned a sense, by no means disquieting, of the disequilibrium that exists between the demands of a syllabus and the achievement required to pass in the corresponding test. To qualify in a course of study did not require fulfilment of the conditions or of the apparent designs of that course in a sense even approximately complete. Here was a chance of life! In how many of my subsidiary subjects did I not, in students' jargon, 'scrape through' on a minimum along with the majority of my peers!

Youthful idealism underwent a gradual disillusionment as one realized that this was 'college'. Yet one was innocent of revolt. All this business was going to lead somewhere. One's teachers seemed to think it would. One's companions, when it occurred to

them, seemed to think it would. Like most of them I was punctual, attentive, burdened, perplexed, expectant—eager for the points, *résumés*, formulas, synopses to be extracted from cribs, text-books and lecture-notes. Never did a neophyte of learning respond more devoutly to the sundry helps in diverse places dispensed by that impersonal Providence whose tabernacles have increased and prospered with the spread of universities like our own. And few could have been more impatient at such departures as the officiating priest might make from the consecrated modes of dispensation. Lectures, I agreed, must be on the syllabus; and questions should be related to both. Herford put Raleigh in the shade, Faguet outshone Sainte-Beuve, because in each case the former appeared to have written with an eye to the syllabus.

For three or four years I worked consistently, conscientiously, laboriously, thwarted by much ill-health, but spurred by the salutary assurance that I should be unable to face the final test without exhausting, if not exhaustive, preparation, and invariably the test confirmed my assurance. The harder I had worked—straining the limits of my modest, hampered abilities and using every trick or tip I could honestly come by in order to be equal with the examiner— the better the result. Cumbrous preparation was my equivalent for what others called 'examination luck'—stolid application streaked with flights of fascinating things which this was never the time to grasp, but to which I promised myself to return when the race was over.

Now that the laurels are dry I still glance about for those glamorous wings, like an ageing and fanciful jockey going back over the course for the butterflies he might have passed in the heyday of his 'form'. A little of the gold came off in the chase. A sigh or two gone up from the souls of the poets, slaughtered in our examination papers, resound in my ears, to this day. From forgotten perturbations over an 'exact context' lingers only

> Ariane, ma sœur, de quel amour blessée
> Vous mourûtes au bord où vous fûtes laissée?

The popularity of these lines shows, I think, what was wrong. We were always looking for details that seemed to us romantic in the French classical dramatists. Their works were moreover too indifferently presented to make any specific impression on our minds. To this day I doubt whether the spirit of Racine's plays can

be 'got over' by a British lecturer to an audience of undergraduates Neither Racine nor Corneille was an 'experience' to me at this stage. An incurable sense of conventionality blocked any emotional or aesthetic contact with them. Nor was the greatness of Molière perceived, although what comedies of his we read presented no comparable difficulty. The whole of French classicism left us cold. It was too much like Boileau's *Art Poétique*, which I read more easily because it was a clear, if uninteresting, argument. What chance had its rational pseudo-cantos of being taken seriously by youths who were imbibing Shelley's *Defence*? The truth is that the study of the French classics demanded more mature minds than ours and more attention than our teachers had time—even if they had the taste—to give.

*
*   *

It is hard to ascertain what permanent gains accrued from the four subsidiary subjects taken along with French. After four years in desultory or concentrated pursuit of Latin (counting those of my schooling in the subject), after three consecutive sessions at German,* after a couple of years' courses in English and the course in Economics, I confess that I retained from these studies nothing that could be called a reliable acquisition. A genuine foretaste of the savour of German lyricism (which appealed to us far more than what French poetry we then knew), a suspicion of what awkward things economics are about, a wish to renew acquaintance with Chaucer, and some notions of a tradition ranging back from Browning to the Venerable Bede—such approximations are surely not all that these courses were designed to provide. As a Latinist I belong to that large class of modern initiates who, confronted in public places with an appeal to translate an inscription, feel vaguely chagrined at being unable to comply. Subsequently I was not able to pursue any of these subsidiary subjects to the point of personal, as distinguished from examinational, proficiency; and I have often wondered what value could be attached to them. I do not like to think they have none. But in the event, the scheme completed, the components seemed to have nothing further to offer. One passed out, sold one's books and counted five towards a qualifying nine.

* The three years included one spent away from College, during which, however, I kept the language going on my own.

CHAPTER SIX

A CHANGE FOR THE BETTER

THE genial spirit of the College and the amenities of its surroundings had already begun to compensate for what embarrassments the scheme of studies had imposed on a novice so ill prepared as myself. But before coming to the brighter side, I must attempt to complete the specific account of undergraduate education as I experienced it towards the end of the first decade of this century.

Soon after the interview described at the beginning of the last chapter, I was taken aside by a senior student of the French department who enquired how I had fared. My interrogator was the youngest of three brothers who hailed from my home town. Two of them rose to intellectual eminence and he was himself of a scholarly disposition. On hearing that my consultation with the Head of the department had, as I thought, gone fairly well, the young man warned me with an enigmatic smile that I might find the professor less agreeably disposed when I had become an habitué of his classes.

Tall, distinguished-looking, externally impressive, my first professor of French gave an undeniable example of strenuous devotion to scholarship. But his attitude to his students could degenerate into that of an academic slave-driver, more anxious to sustain his reputation as a trainer in the race for high places on the Honours list than to impart enlightenment on the spirit of the texts appointed for study.

From their first week in the fold the professor's 'lambs' (as the group of my year came to be called since we were often 'slaughtered') found they were expected to memorize and apply a linguistic skill of which they knew nothing to the dismemberment of a few of the finest productions of early French literary genius which they had had no time to read as such. From an aesthetic standpoint the results were of course squalid.* The air of esoteric authority with which these impositions were professed was reinforced by the most marked tones of *grasseyement* that have ever rattled the drums of

---

* I have described some of them in a chapter called 'French before Sunrise' in *The Assault on French Literature*, Manchester, 1963.

my ears. Our small classroom shook with the vibrations of the guttural *r*'s, and for one *éleve* (still fleeing from the Wrath to Come) the word *par-r-r-role* resounded as if pronounced by an angry deity amidst the thunders of the Last Day.

Doom was postponed. By another of those strokes of luck that have enlivened my progress through the maze of modern studies, a new appointment removed our formidable dominie at the end of my first year. We returned to find the department in the charge of a short, square-shouldered Frenchman with an Assyrian beard and a blue-black *mèche*, who spoke a language that at first we could hardly make out. It was French. An obscure period ensued during which, for the lower classes, the newcomer had to risk lecturing in English. If from this early stage of his teaching I recall a phrase, it is not to caricature an accent somewhat removed from normal usage but to disclose the way his mind worked: 'We *have* seen this before; we *weel* see it again.' The Sorbonne of his time (and of the year I was to spend there a decade and a half later) was in its Faculté des Lettres addicted, one might say dedicated, to the cult of influence and derivations. Literary phenomena were far more often 'explained' in terms of what they had developed from or into than appraised for what they were. Before he died, the distinguished *comparatiste*, Paul Hazard, admitted: 'Il n'y a plus de professeurs de lettres.'

No doubt this method supplied foundations to literary studies of a solidity they had lacked when works were simply 'appreciated' in the emotional manner of many nineteenth-century critics. But the characteristic defect of the literary historians was their failure effectively to differentiate the spirit of the piece of literature they were striving to 'place' in the stream of 'evolution' that preceded and followed its appearance. The essence often escaped the hand that trapped the influence. If this reservation was partially true of my new teacher, how much more closely would it not apply to his assiduous pupil, who not long afterwards was to be scoffed at for producing exercises of the type properly caricatured by Bruce Truscot as 'Jones in France'. But I anticipate . . .

Professor André Barbier was not a fanatic for any part of the subject he had to present. His academic qualifications were modest and if he ever devoted himself to research, none of it was published. He was, however, an amiable man of broad culture and methodical

habits of thought and work. His interests seemed more varied than his predecessor's, revealing a sense of recent French developments which was quite new to us. If he did not add much to the total of scholarship, he was a good guide to what had been done in many fields. His tutorials in *thème* and essay-writing, when he marked his Honours students' exercises individually, were superior to any correction of the kind I had known. Unlike my previous teachers of the language he did not rely on printed fair copies so highly priced as to keep them out of the reach of pupils and students. Classroom lecturing was not, however, his forte. He did not indulge in the habit of dictating notes, but his mode of discussion was desultory and the interest of his hearers, if not his own, could flag. It may well be that having come to a department with only one assistant to share the work, he found himself at first overwhelmed by the demands of the syllabus. Yet he was seriously disposed to his students, and to any of them who proceeded to specialize he could give much support. I owe him almost everything a novice in literary research could expect from his director of studies. And although the subject he suggested—the influence of Whitman on the Symbolists, upon which he insisted despite appeals from his colleagues as well as from myself—proved too arduous for a beginnner to investigate with success, it led ultimately to some of the liveliest literary interests and contacts that I knew in early life.

The best of what I owe to Professor Barbier had nothing to do with the course prescribed for the degree by his predecessor and which, naturally, could not be altered for those of us now in midstream. Many of the chosen texts were in poetic form; but the earliest of them we had been led to approach without the remotest trace of sensibility, and respectable modern poetry finished for our first professor with the strict Parnassians. It required a revolution to break through these restrictions, and for what happened gratitude must be recorded to Madame André Barbier as well as to the Professor. Very soon their home in North Road became a Mecca of enlightenment and inspiration for those who were frequent callers. And when the able but afflicted Frenchman, Léon-Pierre Marchand, had joined the group from Berck-Plage, daily conversation resounded with the names of Claudel, Péguy, Jammes, Verlaine, Rimbaud, Mallarmé and Valéry.

Before Professor Barbier's régime had lasted a term an obscure

but menacing deterioration in health obliged me to leave College. The not unexpected breakdown had come, precipitated by a course of gymnastic exercises recommended by a good friend as a possible cure. Soon after I reached home my father accompanied me to London to consult a specialist. I believe it was Dr. Robert Hutchinson of Guy's who, after examination, assured us that no vital organ appeared to be affected. The fashionable diagnosis for digestive disorders was Arbuthnot Lane's insistence on the prevalence of *viscera optosis*. My condition was thought to conform and a belt was prescribed for which I was fitted before leaving London. This unsufferable *carcan* I endured for a few years without the remotest benefit. But the relief prompted by the negative verdict persuaded me that life might still be worth living, and for the summer term I returned to Aberystwyth to attend a few classes without resuming the course.

To this simple outline could be added confessions of frustration, anxiety and distress that have persisted through the years with only gradual diminution and with little practical help from sympathetic but mystified doctors. I tell them I have sufficient faith in life to think that, could they contrive me a second spell, my disabilities might be rectified by the end of it. Meanwhile I have subsisted on the beneficence of patient, devoted but equally mystified friends, since the day when a distinguished home-townsman, the late Henry Howells, overtook me walking disconsolately along the Parade and, in words of encouragement, recalled his own plight sixty years earlier, when his life had been threatened with what seemed an incurable ailment. His 'condition' must have been more of a menace than mine, but at least it had a name.

To revert to my main theme I must now adopt a by-path. Like the majority of children we knew, my sister and I had received piano lessons from the time our parents (thanks to my mother's economies) had managed to procure a small upright piano. Through the stimulating attentions of a good teacher I had become attached to the instrument as a source of interest and relaxation and also, it must be confessed, as an absorbent of sentiment and an excuse for histrionics. But it was on returning to Aberystwyth that my real introduction to music in its richness and variety began. This was the gift of one person who, acting independently of the long established but then decadent school of music, brought chamber music home to many of

us in something of its intimacy and charm. Our benefactress has
already been introduced. Madame Barbier had studied at the
Conservatoire under Vincent d'Indy. By her personal energies and
initiative the trite precincts of the College hall, which had hitherto resounded to the voices of special lecturers, the addresses of divines and
the echoes of our amateur concerts and dramatics, suddenly awakened to the rhythms of masterpieces performed by an élite of
Parisian *artistes* transported as if by magic into our midst. And if the
magic was primed by the generosity of those illustrious benefactresses,
the Ladies of Llandinam, it was Madame who acted as impresario
and achieved the miracle of presenting some of the leading French
executants to student audiences in the 'College by the sea'.

One of these musical occasions is unlikely to pass from my
memory. Having returned, without much improvement in health,
I managed to crawl down to the concert hall where from seven until
ten I sat in a state of perhaps pathological elation: one of an audience
who were said to have been as inspiring in their vivid responses to
the musicians' efforts as these were to the unspoilt appreciation of
their juvenile hearers. It is a typical, though not, I fear, a flattering
witness to the quality of my taste at the time that I was swept to the
utmost heaven of delight by a rendering of the two *Légendes* of Liszt.
I have confessed to an early *penchant* for rhetoric. The immense
technical display of the performance held me fascinated. The
visible beauty of the artist, his digital ingenuity and brio, counted
for as much in the impression as the triumphant struggle of the
Saint, miraculously heard above, through and underneath the
extravaganza of the storm. I can still plainly see the wasp-like waist,
the flying mane and coat-tails as the pianist leapt at the keyboard,
gathering the vast chaos of storm sounds into that final crescendo
with which the victorious old mystic mounts the distant shore—the
shore so long, so ingeniously defended by Hell's fury against the
intervention of divine consolation. And I recognize in this vivid
recollection the inveterate response to what I have always found
irresistible in Romantic art, however wildly or grossly expressed—
whether in Byron or Hugo, in Liszt or Wagner—that sense of
man grappling with the hostile forces of nature and fighting
through his fate. This was for me a romantic occasion *par excellence*,
comparable only to my first hearing of *Parsifal* at the Paris Opera
house not long afterwards. Never was the taunt that Romantic

art produces impure reactions, that in it the aesthetic experience is mixed up with Heaven knows what alloy of associated emotions, more justified than in my own case. But I cannot forget the thrill. And I would sometimes give much to regain it now when my friends assure me that my taste has so much improved.

Years afterwards I was told that the pianist of this occasion had smashed the Marquess of Anglesey's piano a few nights later with a repetition of St. Vincent's exploits. But it must not be thought that programme music was Madame Barbier's ideal. Cortot when he came made no effort to stir the gods with imitative thunders. And Madame when she sang César Franck, for instance, adopted no histrionic tone or attitude. Most often she accompanied at these public concerts to which we students were admitted for half-a-crown the series! Nor was this the limit of her generosity. Throwing the partition of her drawing-room open, she encouraged us to come to hear the classical symphonies arranged for two pianos played by herself and Dr. Schott, F.R.S., the professor of applied mathematics. A blackboard inscribed with the movements was placed between the instruments and, after a few words of introduction from the Doctor, the executants would start on their sonorous journey, mitigating nothing in sound, speed or *da capo* repetitions. Meanwhile on the other side of the wall in a small sanctum of his own Professor Barbier would be correcting the week's consignment of exercises, his raven hair a trifle disordered but his patience, and the smoke-rings ascending from his pipe, unruffled by the torrents of percussion taps raining down on the keyboards in the next room.

To several of us Madame Barbier gave piano lessons free. Mine were few and sporadic, but they instilled a corrective or two. Hardly had I touched a note on the first occasion when she threw up her arms in protest: 'Trop d'émotion! trop d'émotion!' The words bring me to my most pretentious confession: my consent to open a students' concert in the College hall with a pianoforte solo. The mixture of nervousness and vanity that swept my soul on this occasion couldn't be described. By dint of plodding application, intermittent bouts of concentration and recapitulation *ad nauseam*, I had committed a few pieces to my uncertain memory and these I would revamp with more effect than fidelity.* Not that I could trust my memory to recall a

---

* What patience our excellent landlady must have had to allow a large new upright to be appropriated solely for our amusement!

single bar; but I hoped my hands would carry me through by the 'feel'. What they felt, however, as soon as my toes touched a pedal of the College Bechstein was an uncanny shift of the keyboard that threatened to throw me off my beat. Not to risk too much, I skipped the first movement of Mendelssohn's *Rondo Capriccioso* and plunged into the second, watching the agility of my own fingers and praying Almighty God to keep them on the keys and propel them on to the big chords of the coda. Crash, bang, they arrive, sustained by an unrelinquished loud pedal until the uproar blends with the applause of an audience more surprised than impressed by this show of acrobatics from a person who seemed to be dying of languor.

The next morning my good friend, Quayle, led the rest of the boarders into the breakfast room at Aubrey House to announce that the London papers had reported my performance . . . That was how I came to buy my first daily newspaper—unfortunately the wrong one. Nor was this the end of the affair. Rumours of those crashed chords pursued me when, years later, I went to live and work in Snowdonia. Still at odd moments they waylay my peregrinations with the tenacity of those sins that ultimately find you out.

Enlargement of one's musical horizons was by no means the only boon afforded by Madame Barbier's salon. It was there I picked up my first notions of the Symbolists whose poems excited comments not entirely free from criticism. It would have been too hazardous for the professor to bring them into the course whose prescriptions still ended on the safe side of 1870. But when in my Honours examination I faced the Essay paper I was pleased to find that it contained a subject involving comparisons between the Symbolists and the Parnassians. This I attacked with fervour, fluency and assurance. On reaching home, however, misgivings arose. Mine was probably the first answer written in praise of the Symbolists in a Welsh Honours examination. But had I not given all the virtues of the Symbolists to the Parnassians and all the failings of the Parnassians to the Symbolists? In my dejection I risked a hasty note to my professor imploring him to sort things out.

I had worked my Honours papers with an infernal pain in my side. A month later it was diagnosed as appendicitis. The next morning my harassed mother brought up to my bedroom a postcard signed 'A.B.' It announced that I had been given a 'first'. The symptoms vanished.

With preparation for Honours the strain consequent upon the earlier pressure of ill-assorted disciplines had begun to relax. Issues became clearer; interest as distinct from application revived; contact with my teachers was possible and helpful. Having a preference for specialization which all undergraduates do not share (and there will be a much greater number who don't in future), I found concentration easier in accordance with a better integrated syllabus whose parts, though still diverse, were more helpfully related to one another.

The distinctive reading for the Honours course was mainly prescribed from the earlier phases of French literature and presented with effects I have described elsewhere.* For me the old French texts were spoiled by too much insistence on etymological detail. I found relief in the prescribed selections from the Renaissance poets to which I became genuinely attached. Here my regular and stimulating tutor was Emile Faguet whose well known collection of essays, conversational but not desultory, on Rabelais, Ronsard, Du Bellay and Montaigne put some of the most fascinating writers of France within the orbit of interest of thousands in my time. Montaigne's essay *L'Institution des Enfants* became a life-long favourite from the moment it enlightened me on what was wrong with the course, wrong too with a large part of university education, from that day to this—the tendency to overcharge the memory at the expense of training the judgement.

This fault, moreover, was the inevitable consequence of what I believe to be the flaw in the Honours system as maintained in British universities, namely the conception of the course as a preparation for a competitive examination. The spirit of competition, while it may stimulate the slothful student to ephemeral activity and can precipitate success upon embarrassed recipients, is a dubious concomitant to attentive studies and a probable distraction to the development of real understanding. For me at least what pensive joys the course might have fostered were largely held off by the scarecrow of results. Upon them hung my future in a sense which for reasons already adumbrated appeared exclusive. A good Honours degree or nothing ahead seemed the alternatives. And even now I do not think I was mistaken. Yet the result, when it

* See *The Assault on French Literature*, Chapter II.

came, brought the not unpleasant shock which people of a certain
temperament experience when they receive more than they expect.

*

*   *

If I have been severe, perhaps too severe, on the teaching side of
College life, one of my concerns has been to distinguish it from the
true life of the College, the life the students themselves had created
(with the concurrence of an amiable staff and a friendly administra-
tion) and maintained with that devotion, that genius British students
have always shown for large-scale social institutions. The system of
diversions, conventions and amenities that had grown up with
generations of our predecessors I find difficult to characterize
adequately, even in the critical perspective of half-a-century. It
would be impossible to do so without admitting its humorous
weaknesses and odd shortcomings. But to concentrate on these
would be to underestimate something to which most of us owed a
considerable amount of our social education, and that many of us
still revere in retrospect. It was essentially a type of *esprit de corps*,
liberal in intention, though not without restrictions and formalities,
which reigned on the whole happily, if sometimes a little heavily,
over our undergraduate existence both in its communal and in its
intimate aspects.

The communal life was shared under strict conditions by almost
equal numbers of both sexes and offered a pattern of behaviour of
which most of our schools had presented no model. I was sufficiently
uncouth to derive from it the earliest of whatever lessons in *savoir
vivre* I had learnt since boyhood. Before long the social side had so
much endeared the place to me that I should have felt it a calamity
to be obliged to leave immediately after the three years' minimum
required for graduation.

Looked at a little more curiously, however, our life at Aberystwyth
assumes the form of a closed community with laws, mostly unwritten,
and conventions of a special and exclusive character, some of them
so local in their origin and application as to be quite inadaptable
to the requirements of society in the world without. They were the
conventions of a class of adolescents who were at once uncommonly
free from restraint and yet curiously restricted. The contradiction

belonged to the kind of conventionality I had known in the chapel
circles of my boyhood. Indeed there was more than a savour of
nonconformity about the rule of life that reigned in our beloved
Thelema. *Fais ce que vouldras* might have been written over its
doors, but Heaven help you if you persisted in doing anything of
which the majority disapproved!

Unfortunately the majority could be dominated by a noisy
element. A jovial species of hooliganism was ever ready to disrupt
what efforts were made at social or artistic expression. This was
particularly prominent on public occasions. Societies flourished,
the small ones sedately, the larger uproariously. That sociable but
suspect amenity, the dance, was forbidden by order. Gala nights
passed gaily for the initiates with concerts, whist and dramatics,
interspersed with scrambles for refreshments, pompous speechifica-
tions, lingering *tête-à-tête* on the balcony or in the tower. Lurking in
the background bands of the unattached punctuated the proceedings
with choruses and cat-calls. At a hint of sandwiches and coffee
they descended upon Rome. No-one demurred; it was part of the
show. Authority stepped in to prevent escort when the show was
over. How many hearts must have bled with humiliation at having
to part company at the College portal under that icy vigilance,
determined to bar the probabilities of protracted meanderings
beside a soothing or a too inspiring sea!

It is remarkable what power a relatively small group whose
standards are low, but whose voices are loud, can exercise over a
company of well mannered people. The reign of Demos at
Aberystwyth was in my days a phenomenon that has often since
occupied my thoughts. Harmless in intention, it was the vicious
counterpart of what we considered the proudest asset in our
communal life, its corporate spirit. We acted together; we were
expected to act together; we were sometimes forced to act together
against the wish of individuals or of minorities. When, however,
one of these minor groups had the physical strength to impose its
will, this became perforce the will of the rest of us. So that, despite
a cult of unconventionality, much in our customs and many of our
functions implied an attitude of subservient conformity against which
more than one person must, I assume, have felt himself in irritable
but impotent revolt. Strange are the uses of adversity! Without
this brush with experience should I ever have understood how

easily democracy can become a despotism, or how the French Revolution rapidly degenerated into a tyranny? But these are odious comparisons. What there was of mob rule at Aberystwyth was an easy if not enlightened despotism. Its decrees were unwritten laws assimilated into our modes of life as if from time immemorial. Only on rare occasions did its will become articulate; but then it could be unspeakably intolerant.

Needless to say the social side of our life had obvious virtues. The best, although this implies the worst that could be said of it, is that it was *not* a hotbed of individualism. On the contrary it was on the whole a healthy and an easy camaraderie—idealistic, with much of that disinterested friendliness which makes the communities of youth so often spiritually superior to those of their elders. Not suspicion or hostility, but welcome and cordiality were its marks, and these were evinced from the first. It struck me as delightful that newcomers were not persecuted in the manner habitual in similar institutions where there are graded years. It is not to be wondered at that we loved the place or the life or one another or ourselves, so positive a note of appreciation and good will was maintained and so winning the example many of our seniors scrupulously set us. That this could be accompanied by no little self-consciousness has to be admitted, but as an afterthought, lest what was good in our relationships should now appear to be idealized in retrospect. One of the most remarkable features of the life was the almost total absence of snobbery. In the general under-estimate of intellectual values—more an unfortunate pose than a radical state of mind—intellectual snobbery had no possible chance of showing itself, and social snobbery would have been scoffed out of countenance, at least among the men with whom it was my luck to associate.

With the women it may have been different.

My first soirée had been an intimidating affair. Cautiously perambulating the covered quadrangle which was the hub of our social universe, I had been seized by a conscientious steward whose female counterpart had pounced on another unprepared victim to whom I found myself callously introduced. The young woman was obviously appalled at her fate and hastened to conceal her partner in a corner of the balcony above the throng, while she improvised plans for escape. What about whist? But surely the

drive was finishing! An acute silence followed my observation and I was forced to yield. We entered to await the arrival of another couple of irreconcilables who, of course, never turned up.

Tired of avoiding each other's gaze, we drifted out again to the balcony, where my agony of suspense was consummated. Over the bridge of her nose the almost stationary hands of the College clock moved to laconic ticks, recalling the gloomiest sermon of my youth, that of the static dial of Hell. Eternity had not begun.

*

*   *

I once heard a distinguished Oxford scholar complain that his university gave no adequate training in research method. A comparable reservation was made by Abraham Flexner over thirty years ago: 'The provincial universities provide only incidentally for graduate work.' Proper supervision would have required larger staffs than most universities could afford, so that either the professor could be liberated for this work or a director could be appointed to take charge of post-graduate studies.

Without such help most young graduates embarked upon their tasks not only with insufficient technical preparation but with an outlook too narrow and a judgement too immature for an immediately successful prosecution of their objectives. A training which had been mainly a drill in assimilation could not be considered a satisfactory qualification for the kinds of operation involved in the pursuit of what was distinguished as 'original research.' Without perhaps suspecting the deficiencies of his undergraduate equipment the prospective researcher might settle down to a job which circumscribed him within a narrow field or exiled him to a remote corner of a wide one. The choice once made, his fate was for the time fixed. The energy with which he concentrated on his task might in the end betray him. Not infrequently commendable application produced a narrow crank from whom it was hopeless to expect an imaginative presentation of a subject either in its broad generality or in its illuminating detail, because the imagination that generalizes or illuminates, if it had been there to start with, had not been sufficiently cultivated. Nothing might be there before long but a fanatic's proficiency in an unrelated technique. This man

might be good at phonetics just as another was good at carburettors. 'The parallel is exact,' said Newman eighty years ago. 'As the body may be sacrificed to some manual or other toil, whether moderate or oppressive, so may the intellect be devoted to some specific profession, and I do not call *this* culture of the intellect.'

It is an honourable thing, of course, that a man should be good at his profession and a modest thing that he should not claim that his profession qualifies him to discourse on the universe. But there is a way of reducing an arts subject to a narrow science with results that are disastrous for the general culture of the person who concentrates solely on his technique, and with consequences which can be more unfortunate still for those whom he may be appointed to instruct.

Against the tendency to introduce the novice into a technical field immediately upon completion of Honours, I submit the following consideration. All research worthy of the name should entail diverse and circumstantial reading. The danger is that often much of this may lead off the main line of interest into byeways and dead-ends, pursued with meagre or negative results. Files of newspapers, for instance, may have to be minutely searched with the doubtful satisfaction that when they have provided nothing they have at least been cleared out of the investigator's path. Time expended in this way need not be counted lost for the experienced researcher. But in the case of a young person whose object is a postgraduate degree, one is tempted to ask whether he could not be better employed than he often is, by being set a task which would extend his knowledge of the history or the scholarship of a subject, or one which, while it initiates him to methods of specialization, might also improve his judgement and his taste by facilitating contact with some of the many masterpieces his previous studies will have had to ignore.

Apart from a total lack of technical equipment and of good method, which I expect I shared with most young graduates of my time, the chief difficulties I had to face when beginning independent work were of a more modest order. It would be unjust to blame my education entirely for the condition I found myself in at this juncture. Yet it will, I think, be admitted that, whatever it had done for me hitherto, the types of training I have described had not enabled or encouraged me to express myself either freely or correctly in English. It was during what I hesitate to call my first 'research years'

that I felt most keenly this disability. It was then I discovered that, almost literally, I possessed no language. The business of expressing a thing clearly in accurate words placed in regular or effective order had almost entirely to be learnt. I shall always appreciate my initial efforts at research for teaching me this. I, who could entertain the illusion of having something of a 'teeming brain', found myself sitting for hours, unable to compose more than a phrase which would glower at me from the top of a blank sheet like an epitaph of my own invention on the tombstone of my aspirations.

My first attempt to write something to justify the grant I was receiving is a curious memory. For subject I tried my hand at a comparison of Whitman with the Belgian poet, Emile Verhaeren. Despite a number of vague notions floating about in my head, I had no clear idea of what was expected of me, what to leave to the generalizations of the critics, or what to claim as my own findings. And I was disturbed by the disappointment my professor betrayed when he received as first draft a string of balanced quotations. I felt I could not better my authorities' statements except by capping them with illustrations. That done, why invent?

A corollary to this method of juxtaposition may amuse the reader. I had risked including a pair of examples of sexual imagery, one from each poet, and I was surprised to find that the professor (not my own) who edited the essay for *Aberystwyth Studies* had suppressed the example from Whitman! This precaution, however, made it possible for offprints to be sold at the door of the College hall at the close of a lecture delivered by Verhaeren when he came to Aberystwyth in 1915.

For I had been caught by what seemed the most vital and human poetry that was being written in the world at that time. To it I had come through the attempt to find traces of Whitman's influence on the Continent of Europe, encouraged by Stefan Zweig's exciting essay on Verhaeren. A thousand vague but powerful reactions to nature and to modernity, intercepted through the fumes of malady by a religious imagination withdrawn from the religious forms observed in his youth, flashed upon me with an intimate recognition, along with much not so easy to assimilate: the gross vision of Flanders, the excessively morbid emphasis which was sometimes too strong even for my seasoned palate. The hallucinated vision of Industry with its tremendous power, hideously vindictive yet prospectively

beneficient, was an illumination (perhaps a delusion) which lives with me still. And when I passed from this interpretation—stimulating though distorted—of the active present to the aftermath of exultant pantheism expressed in *Les Visages de la Vie* and *La Multiple Splendeur*, I felt for moments lifted through the poets' vision to the perception of a universe, mystically conceived, of self-ordered forces and regnant ideas which seemed at times the fulfilment of all my confused ideals and tortuous aspirations and which, translated into 'sovereign rhythms' by this last of the Romanticists, was to bring the finale of my own romantic enthusiasm to an end. Verhaeren was killed in an accident in 1916. The enthusiastic reception for his poetry that had spread throughout Europe before the war suddenly collapsed and has never revived. I feel this is unjust to a fervent and sympathetic nature who fully perceived the promise of science in his time, even if he failed to appreciate the undiminished virulence of evil waiting to misapply it.

Chapter Seven

PARIS PREWAR

PICTURE a rather impressionable youth who in the winter of 1913-14 set out to discover something about the kinds of free verse then being practised by certain French poets, and who, if he hadn't much success in that quest, picked up a few useful novelties of experience and met a number of very pleasant people. Off he went under the friendliest auspices from his College. Through Sir Edward Anwyl's mediation* he was able to start work at the British Museum with a few words of direction from Ernest Rhys, then editor of the *Everyman* library of publications. Mr. Rhys's name I mention with special gratitude. My plans were to go to Paris at the earliest opportunity and, if possible, to make contact with some of those poets who were still alive enough to represent the fading glories of the Symbolist movement. The problem was how to gain access without appearing to gate-crash.

It was Ernest Rhys who one day, with a rather worried look, breathed the name of Ezra Pound, a poet whose star was already in the ascendant and who had just come back from Paris, where he had seen everyone of importance for the pattern of poetic change. The reason for Mr. Rhys's look of anxiety was, I gathered, the result of Pound's habit of disagreeing with most people around him. Mr. Pound, I was warned, was slightly eccentric, but he was 'the man for me'. I was given his address and advised to tackle him in my own name. I wrote. Nothing happened. That is nothing happened by return of post.

My hopes of hearing from him had been shelved for several days when, late one afternoon, returning to my lodgings in North London, I found a kind of telegram awaiting me. There was sufficient resemblance to my address on the envelope for the missive to have been delivered, but, when opened, the message was, like a true oracular utterance, quite unintelligible. Read right way up or upside down, perused from what appeared to be the beginning or

* Sir Edward was Professor of Celtic, a scholar of varied culture and the most popular member of the staff.

from where things seemed to end, the scrawl remained like a
shattered hieroglyphic in the hands of a grave-digger, and I was
about to throw its fragments into the grave of my aspirations, when
it occurred to me that a man, even an eccentric, even a poet, does
not send a wire for any but immediate purposes. So turning up
Mr. Pound's address I set out, tired as I was after a day's drudgery
at the Museum, in search of No. 11, Church Walk, Kensington.

You have doubtless concluded that our hero was a naïve young
man. There is no plumbing the depths of his naïvety on this occasion,
or of the dreams that passed through his mind in anticipation of
this particular journey's end. He was going to meet his first real
poet, and his private conception of a poet was that he must, before
everything else, be a great gentleman and quite well-to-do. This was
the fault of his excellent education. Ronsard was a gentleman;
Du Bellay was even better born. The two 'Alfreds', Vigny and
Musset, were, as every schoolboy knows, conscious of their lineage.
Even Victor Hugo became a *comte*. I need not remind you that
almost every great English poet was born, bred or buried a
gentleman. Think of Byron, Shelley or Tennyson. Even Wordsworth,
who once roughed it with his sister at Dove Cottage, ended up at
Rydal Mount with a sinecure like the Postmaster General's in
his desk and several ladies at hand to copy out the various mss. of
the *Prelude* . . . And here was I going to call upon one such as they,
at quite a good address near Kensington Church.

The Church was wrapping itself up in the gloom of a winter's
evening when I emerged from the tube station. I can well remember,
as I crossed into the churchyard, looking round for the lofty façade
behind which the poet would be ensconced reading Villon or
Cavalcante or Alain Chartier or Dante, if he were not more
seriously engaged in writing immortal verse. But no impressive
residence came to meet my inquiring gaze. I walked on, following a
constable's instructions and nervously fingering the telegram, my
Open Sesame, screwed up in my pocket. Lower and lower my
spirits sank as I strode from one end of the graveyard to the other,
in search of Church Walk.

It couldn't be this scowling little court dimly outlined on my left?
Yes; 'Church Walk' was just visible above me, glimmering like
those fatal words, 'Abandon hope!' No. 11, the poet's abode,
must be hereabout. I crept from door to door, from no. 1 to no. 10;

then came 12 and of course 13. Was I the victim of a practical joke?
A final inspection of the dingiest corner revealed the two ones.
More in disgust than timidity I tapped the shabby door. Presently
there was a shuffle within and the door came slowly ajar. An
unpropitious visage outlined itself between door and doorframe
and responded to my question by disappearing, soon however to
return. Mr. Pound was in: I must follow upstairs. I followed.
A bedroom door opened upon a curious scene: a bare little room
furnished with orange-boxes, books cascading over them and
everywhere else, and in the middle of the den an iron bedstead, and
on the bed, like a Sultan on his couch, there sat one of the most
handsome men I had ever set eyes on—none other than the versatile,
voluble, vainglorious, vituperative Ezra Pound.

Sultans apparently don't rise to greet callers. I was waved in the
direction of a lesser orange box, and the consultation, or rather the
monologue, began. Mr. Pound *had* been in Paris, had met the
writers I wanted to meet and was generous with addresses and
advice. One piece of advice stuck in my mind and turned out to be
more reasonable than you would suppose: 'Don't go mugging
round the Bibliothèque Nationale.' The French National Library
was to be a frequent haunt in the next few weeks. But the hint to
call upon the poets themselves was an excellent alternative because
they were French poets and wonderfully easy and helpful to talk to,
and none of the Parisian libraries turned out to have more than a
few of their works.

Pungent, racy, sometimes a trifle salacious, the monologue was
still in full spate when I rose to leave. It stopped abruptly when I
asked for an autograph. Striding to the door my interlocutor called
for a carving knife. This made me feel distinctly uneasy. I hadn't
brought weapons myself. But with the large knife in one hand Mr.
Pound didn't measure my throat with the other but seized one of a
pile of discarded volumes containing some of his own poems and
six others, being the entire *oeuvre* of T. E. Hulme. Then with a
sweeping gesture Mr. Pound carved some advertisements out of the
back and signing the copy with an illegible flourish, he handed it to
his visitor who disappeared downstairs more rapidly than he had
come up.

Mr. Pound had provided some addresses of the right people to
see when I reached Paris, and a start was made by calling on Georges

Duhamel then resident in that popularly picturesque street, the rue Mouffetard. From him I secured a few more introductions to colleagues of his, including a coveted one to Verhaeren.

I'm afraid I took for granted the responses that awaited my persistent inquiries, tiresome enthusiasms and considerable ignorance. The appeals I made for clues and guidance got receptions which, though modest in comparison with those of an expert interviewer, have always seemed to me generous. Subsequent efforts, anyhow, have never been able to recapture the vivacity of those talks. Not that Frenchmen of letters have become less affable since the first World War. Perhaps it is simply that youth makes a better audience than maturity, especially for members of a race with a genius for expansiveness, so often checked by that *froideur*, that *morgue* which remains the conventional attitude of the seasoned Britisher abroad.

But there is doubtless another explanation of the ease with which conversations started. Academic as was the form of my inquiries, they were anything but remote from the interests of most of my interlocutors. Here I must do justice to my professor's choice of subject. Everyone I met having pretensions to an interest in contemporary poetry was more or less aware of the main objects of my quest—Whitman's influence and the development of the *vers libre*. Free verse seemed to be the quarry of every living poet—or his *bête noire*. As for Whitman, while each poet denied his influence, few were averse to invoking it in the case of a colleague, though the motive for this may have been the wish to help an anxious young foreigner with a possible hint of copy.

It would be presumptuous to assume that most of the writers I met early in 1914 would be metaphorically worth introducing to readers of this book. Anyone curious about them or interested in the questions on which I tried to get some light might turn to a collection of essays and interviews which appeared in 1951.* Here I will simply recall three talks which did not involve technicalities.

Just before I set out Madame Barbier had given me a word of introduction to a minor poet called André Spire. My memory has always been liable to confuse proper names, and during a protracted search for M. Spire's address a more important name supplanted the one I had been given. The confusion persisted until I had called at the residence of André Gide and deposited the

* *The Background of Modern French Poetry*, Cambridge University Press.

lady's card. Late that night I came to my senses and immediately scribbled a couple of apologies. Sharp reproaches ensued from the lady across the Channel. But their asperity was softened by a delicate little note that preceded them from Gide himself, pretending he was pleased with my blunder and inviting me to meet him. I distinctly remember how the chalk-like palor of his face contrasted with the clerical black of the clothes he wore, the lank hair under the broad black felt and the slowness and care of his speech. He seemed to withdraw in thought as he spoke. Our rendezvous was the then diminutive office of the *Nouvelle Revue française* which Gide had recently helped to found, and there he persuaded someone in authority to place back numbers of the review at my disposal. It was a person whose appearance I remember as attractive—an extraordinarily intelligent face lit with dark lustrous eyes. It may have been Jacques Rivière.

Gide gave me a card for Valéry Larbaud whose interest in Whitman was explicit. The afternoon I called he had just returned from a cruise in the Mediterranean. In an apartment of minute proportions he prepared and served some distinctly thin China tea, clotted with cream, which we sipped as a dissolvent to rolls of a granite like texture unearthed from a cupboard where they must have matured since my host's departure for his cruise. I seem to retain nothing more of his interview except a copy of *Barnabooth* containing *poésies* in free verse which show signs of a close emulation of Whitman's rhythms and mannerisms.

The most exciting of these visits I have yet to recall.

It was bright and keen the morning I set out to see Verhaeren. After what seemed an endless climb I found his flat in a row of villas on the hill-top of Saint-Cloud. The room I was shown into opened on another, where two men sat at a table strewn with the remains of a meal. One of them turned a strange but familiar visage in my direction and dashed forward with an impetuous welcome. 'Je vais vous enfermer!' was his second thought. The partition was closed with a bang and I was left a prisoner. Suddenly the whirlwind reappeared: 'Here's something to read.' A batch of journals and reviews was shed by a vanishing hand, and again I was alone. I had time to glance at two or three large portraits of the poet which seemed, for all their impressionistic vivacity, far less alive than the image I had just perceived.

Verhaeren's appearance at this time, and indeed throughout his maturity, was unique.* Broadly built but meagre and under the middle height, he had, with his drooping shoulders, lean limbs and haggard features, almost the appearance of a broken man. His strong, tanned face was gnarled and furrowed like the bark of a tree: there was sometimes the suggestion of a faun about him, as he moved with his strange look of hallucination accentuated by his jerky, rustic gait. But a warmth of greeting shone from the dark, wild eyes and encouragement beamed in the expansive smile! Not that his joyous, nervously excitable manner could conceal the lasting stigmata of those abnormal ecstasies of pain and joy through which his soul had passed. Nor could the mirth in his eyes efface the desolate, dreaming sadness—that interminable 'vista' look—which was their wonted expression and which seemed to persist in the deep furrows of the face, in the pendulous locks of iron-grey hair and in the heavy droop of the huge brown moustaches: the eyes, the hair of a Viking gazing through the wide, sad mists of modern wisdom, back to the primal sanities of an unremembered yet haunting pre-existence.

From imaginary portrait painting I was recalled to realities by a second welcome as volcanic as the first. When its tremors had subsided I found myself seated near the poet, who had begun to talk. I could not keep my eyes off him. A short green dressing-jacket with pale blue collar and cuffs, orange socks and downtrodden scarlet slippers composed his morning *négligé*. Now and then he would pause over a thought, drawing his long moustaches through the tapering points of his small, feminine hands, or flattering his thick hair with a nervous palm. Then throwing himself back in his *fauteuil* and putting the tips of his long fingernails together, he would set out on some voyage of reminiscence with just as much fervour, one would think, as he had started with upon the adventure itself.

His visits to England he recalled with delight. I believe he would have rehearsed them till nightfall, but that with despicable persistence, I kept dragging him back to the minutiae upon which I had come to be informed. His patience was inexhaustible. He would take up my dry little points, blow the dust off them and hand them back with a glint of significance, as if to persuade me that they were

* This paragraph comes from my first book on Verhaeren, now out of print.

not so worthless after all. That was it: significance everywhere, burning up the dross of the dingiest realities.

Reluctantly I rose to leave. Verhaeren accompanied me to the stairs with 'Au revoir—pas adieu!' As I descended, I caught a last glimpse through the chink of the door: 'Quand vous reviendrez à Paris . . .' It was in Wales I saw him next, driven like a leaf before the full blast of war.

The Alma Mater of those days thought it somewhat of an adventure for a graduate of 24 to go to Paris on his own, and care had been taken to place him under the right auspices and to find him a *pension* that would be quite *comme il faut*. Only my father with his direct Welsh humour refused to take these solemn precautions seriously. As we parted at his shop-door the two words of advice he pronounced with a twinkle were not to spend too much time at the Folies Bergères and to beware of the *apaches*. Follies of the expensive kinds I have usually found beyond my means. As for my brush with the *apaches*, I will come to that later.

In the train from Calais to Paris I had found myself seated in front of a stranger with whom a few words were exchanged on approaching our destination. He was a German who evidently thought himself informed about differences between family life in France and in England, and he took care to impress upon me that I should find nothing like 'home' in Paris. From the moment of my arrival, however, this chill prediction was belied. At a small flat *au cinquième* in the rue du Vieux Colombier I enjoyed from the first evening what comforts I was used to along with a number of new interests which were French. From my hostess and her relatives with whom I often stayed afterwards I learnt all I have known of middle-class life in France, and this has turned me into a defender of the *bourgeoisie* even against an antagonist as formidable as Flaubert. Many faults and foibles must, I feel, be forgiven a class so reasonably devoted to the good things of life and whose *maîtresses de maison* spent less time on refurbishing corridors and polishing tiles and oilcloth than on the arts of preparing and presenting carefully chosen food and drinks. When Mme David gave a dinner party it was an unforgettable event, not merely because of the excellent fare, but for the sparkle and gaiety of the conversation. And it is horrible to think that having survived the first world war, so much of that

sparkle and gaiety was quenched in the second, and in the most brutal fashion, by deportation and death.

The winter before the war was fairly severe. My health was disastrous and destroyed many of the pleasures of the trip. But illness can breed moods having a queer intensity which normal conditions fail to produce. Suffering intensely from the cold, I received an impression of the gay city that might have been given by a dream capital of Siberia. High black coal-carts pulled by agile *percherons* with astrakhan collars and manned by haunted-looking drivers; business-men's top hats oddly balanced above shoulders loaded with furs as in early illustrations of Bourget's novels: chestnut roasters crouching over their fires at street corners, and my shuddering stroll round to the Place St. Michel where Notre-Dame revealed herself engraved in snow against a black sky at noon, alien, frigid and acutely beautiful—these are glimpses I never forget. Brighter days and walks were to come; and one of them, my first along the Seine, is an exciting memory. Marvels kept springing upon either bank, including the Trocadero, the Eiffel Tower and the Big Wheel. The flying horses of the Pont Alexandre III with those leaping from the roof of the Grand Palais, seemed the acme of decorative art, only less exhilarating than the heroic figures carved on the flanks of the Arc de Triomphe. Shades of the Napoleons and of Walt Whitman, what tastes you inspired in the unsuspecting Celt on his first tour round the capital of beauty!

As for the visual arts, Impressionists and Post-impressionists were still much in evidence in 1914 and it is amusing to think how obscure or ethereal many of their canvasses seemed to be. How earnestly a few of us tried to 'make out' a vast painting in the gallery of Bernheim jeune, hoping to detect something—a *cathédrale engloutie* or perhaps Venus rising through the foam—out of a sea of brush strokes. Back we stepped further and further to focus things aright until an assistant came to warn us of the danger of upsetting another un-fathomable masterpiece in the depths of the shop.

The theatres flourished with little fear of rivalry from the rudimentary films of that day. Apart from a few popular variety halls, and of course *Grand Guignol* and the *cafés chantants*, social comedy and farce were the dominant attractions of the stage. Needless to say the national theatres, the Comédie française and the Odéon, drew large numbers of students, foreigners and native

habitués, to hear the classics. Most of the production would now be called conventional and much of the acting stilted. The delivery was highly rhetorical and intoned to the point of amusing young visitors who understood nothing of what they heard. But it was a novelty to be in the greatest of the world's theatres surrounded by members of a nation of connoisseurs in the arts of the stage, whose attitudes and gestures of critical appreciation or disapproval were themselves worth watching.

And yet, then as now, it was the little experimental theatres, the *théâtres d'avant-garde*, that attracted the intelligentsia of Paris and the cream of foreigners.

The rue du Vieux Colombier where I lodged runs between the rue de Rennes and the Place St. Sulpice. A few yards northward brought one into the Boulevard St. Germain. At this time the Deux Magots and the Café de Flore, though flourishing rendezvous of the better sort, had nothing of the intellectual glamour which the attentions of Sartre and the Existentialists have endowed them with. Montmartre reigned without a rival over the artistic world. In the world of the theatre, however, the old street I lived in had acquired recent renown through a little *avant-garde* playhouse which had adopted its name. The Théâtre du Vieux Colombier was already flourishing on a repertory including novelties, translations and adaptations presented to illustrate a revival of the art of production under the directive genius of Jacques Copeau.

Copeau's theatre I did not contrive to visit nearly so often as I could now wish. Time was short and so were funds, and my main interests lay outside the scope of drama. But his little theatre had a theoretical and cultural mission which it performed through providing lectures by important writers as well as through its repertory. Two *causeries* I heard stand out. One was Gide's on Dostoievsky; the other, on Verhaeren, was delivered by the American-born Symbolist, Francis Vielé-Griffin. Before one of them, while the audience awaited the curtain to rise, a small incident happened on which I should like to dwell for a moment if only to mention the name of one of my most generous supporters, Tancrède de Visan. Having invited me to meet him in the vestibule, on the way to our seats, he introduced me to a scholar who was considered the authority on the nature and development of the *vers libre*. As Robert de Souza, a figure of military cast, rose to bow stiffly, a

monocle glinted before an eye that looked forbidding. It was evident that the stalls of a packed auditorium was not the place to interrogate the man who knew all the secrets of the new rhythms. Unfortunately circumstances prevented my following up this lead. I had to content myself with reading Souza's books, and I still think them worth attention on the subject of *Du Rythme en français*.

Remy de Gourmont was then the leading exponent of Symbolism, but his infirmities kept him a recluse. I succeeded no further with him than an exchange of notes. After Gourmont, Tancrède de Visan was regarded as the best contemporary writer on the movement. His book of essays, *L'Attitude du lyrisme contemporain*, is still, I think, well worth reading as an introduction. To him and to the devoted Whitmanian, Léon Bazalgette, I owe considerable debts of gratitude for guidance and help. Let me recall the impression of Tancrède de Visan, in top hat and frockcoat, climbing the stair-case of no. 13, rue du Vieux Colombier, to show me a few precious copies of the rare Symbolist review, *La Vogue*, wrapped in a news-paper. Or of lunching with Bazalgette at the little *restaurant du Dragon* in the Boulevard St. Germain, his talk fresh with reminiscences of *Leaves of Grass*.

The French undeniably have the arts of explication at their fingertips. Their willingness to expound and exchange ideas can be a boon to beginners; it may constitute a free gift to the foreigner, one that is extremely difficult to repay in one's own country. The ideas one picks up in these interviews may often prove more personal than permanent; but there is always the lesson in the art of discussion —by no means easy to practise in Britain—the skilful use of words and the manipulation of ideas at which the French are the teachers of the world.

During the winter of '13-'14 an item of exceptional interest figured in the repertory of the Opera. *Parsifal* was being presented entire for its first season in France. This chance provided the most memorable operatic event in my experience. I was far from being able to appreciate all that happened in the drama or in the music. But the high moments—such as I thought them to be—were intelligible and very moving in their appeal to ear and eye. The choruses at once captured my Welsh appreciation. Yet it was the wordless episodes that I found most impressive, when the motifs of the music and the acts or gestures on the stage combined to

illustrate the Wagnerian idea of Symbolism. The elevation of the
Grail which as it rose burst into flame and the hero's actions
accompanied only by the musical themes which suggested and
prolonged their significance, these were revelations of the symbolic
powers that can inhere in things seen and heard without their
being made verbally explicit. The lesson of Mallarmé seemed
illustrated and enacted on a grand scale before one's eyes. His
discretion too in pursuit of the demon of analogy was exhibited by
contrast with some of Wagner's 'machinery'. In an early scene the
swan shot by Parsifal fell on the planks with a wooden thud,
destroying for a moment that yearning for the infinite which the
music had begun to express. *Un cygne d'autrefois* incarcerated in his
forgotten lake of ice was something very remote from this.

Another theatrical night must be recalled to strike a balance
between the sublime and the popular. It will doubtless seem a sign
of hoary seniority to be able to affirm that I heard Sarah Bernhardt
of the golden voice in her own theatre. I take the precaution of
adding that, far from seeing the great actress in the full *éclat* of her
prime, the Divine Sarah was far gone in decline by 1914 and it was
rumoured that only improvidence had brought her back to the
footlights. The amount she had spent on pets of all kinds was said
to have ruined her solvency.

It was hard to believe that the actress I saw and heard was in her
seventieth year and that she had acquired an artificial limb. By
adroit manipulations of movement and posture this defect was
skilfully disguised, at least from the eyes of a novice in dramatic
criticism. She had, however, given her age away by accepting for
the first time a role *de femme mûre*. This role was offset by that of a
jeune premier who was obviously another of the lady's pets. The
play itself was sentimental and poor enough to make one sorry to
have surprised a famous actress doing something to make ends meet.
But if the visual aspect of the piece was disappointing one audible
trait commanded attention. The famous *voix d'or* could not be
missed: a little high-pitched, it was clear and melodious as a bell;
its enunciation could be heard without effort at the back of one of the
largest theatres in Europe.

Paris audiences are said to be the most critical in the world. On
this occasion, however, the reaction was an anti-climax. When the
curtain dropped after the last outburst of applause, an effect

supervened the like of which I have never known. The thunderous clapping sank into a kind of *susurrement* like the seething of a hidden sea. I looked over the rail of the *poulailler* down into the pit: the stalls, the balcony, the whole house had succumbed to emotion. Hundreds of handkerchiefs seemed to be fluttering in an ocean of lacrimose adoration. Not wishing to be thrown out as a callous Englishman, I unfolded my handkerchief over the throng. A five-franc note, my last piece of change, shot out to drift like a scrap of flotsam on the ocean of tears.

It was striking midnight when we emerged. The way to the flat lay across the Seine and thence into the Boulevard St. Germain. The night was calm and starlit. Pedestrians were passing along the streets fully illuminated as was the custom before the wars. Our hero sauntered along, his thoughts fixed on what he had seen and heard. Suddenly a grip of iron seized his arm. The paternal warning rang in his ears: the *Apaches*! With a mighty wrench he was free, running along the boulevard for dear life. From a vantage point higher up the thoroughfare he turned to face the brigand defrauded of his prey. No one was coming in his direction. A long way off in the opposite direction a young woman was disappearing with an easy, athletic gait.

The good ladies of no. 13 were anxious to exploit for their *pensionnaire's* benefit as many of the city's attractions as they could procure free tickets for, rearranging the hour of meals to suit the event. Purely for the good of my education they offered to accompany me to a café-concert. One evening after an early dinner we migrated to a haunt on the Grands Boulevards, where we were regaled with some brilliant improvisations interspersed with items of verbal indecency so infantile and flat that I wondered how members of the wittiest nation on earth could have endured them. 'How did you like the show', one of the ladies enquired as we moved out. 'All right', said I innocently. 'But what was that word they used so often beginning with m . . .?'

Judging my audition of French sufficiently improved, they next proposed a special treat for my edification. This was indeed something unique, something which in the event didn't quite come off but which, even as experienced, I wouldn't have missed for all the other initiations of the visit.

At that time Paris was resounding with the reputation of a

professor of philosophy whose lectures at the Collège de France were attracting audiences representing the whole intelligentsia of the capital. In accordance with the demands of fashion as well as of learning, many of those who could be free at one o'clock on the appointed days would contrive to hear Henri Bergson expound his doctrine of the *élan vital*. The distance from the rue du Vieux Colombier to the Collège de France can hardly be more than a kilometre. But after a mid-morning lunch I arrived at the lecture-room, the biggest in the building—to find that not an inch of seating space was visible except in a kind of broad pulpit which contained the lecturer's chair in front of a blackboard. That chair seemed more august than the throne of an archbishop, yet the question was by what kind of vital leap was the philosopher going to reach it. Gangways and side-walks had completely disappeared under the campstools of leisured people who had come too late for a place on the crowded benches. Luckily the double door leading into the lecture-room had glass panels facing the speaker and, in the absence of a janitor, they could be opened a little to allow a precious word or two to pass through.

Tired of waiting I strolled round to another entrance beyond the pulpit to find this one even more thronged. As nothing could be seen of the lecture room from there, I wondered why so many people had gathered in the semi-darkness, when the reason became clear. A stir in the crowd revealed a slight, discreet figure in a neat *redingote* picking his way without ceremony through the mass of students. And now the janitor plays his part. The keys are produced with the usual jangle and, selecting a big one, he unlocks the door. Instantly the pace of events quickens. Up rush the strongest and toughest figures in the throng. Before the door can be locked again they have formed a bodyguard round the lecturer and crushed their way onto the rostrum.

Rushing back to the glass door on the other side of the room I beheld a curious induction ceremony. Bergson was now seated; his rare but fluent gestures had already begun to illustrate the movement of his intuitions. The iron laws of Determinism which had manacled French thought for decades seemed to be yielding to the unpredictable urge of the free spirit of life; while standing up behind the greyhaired magician as many stalwarts as the pulpit could hold were packed round the philosopher in statuesque poses

of respectful attention. With the irrepressible grace that French youths get into their easiest attitudes they remained standing, their black cloaks thrown open, their broad felt sombreros, then fashionable, jammed on the corners of the blackboard. I have often thought of that scene—the maximum of interest and of enthusiasm inspired by a lecturing gift without rhetoric or *grands gestes*, yet spell-binding. I am not aware that any more effective teaching of original thought has been conveyed solely by means of the lecture in my lifetime. How was the effect achieved? The novelty of the subject, the liberation its treatment brought to the mind of its hearers, the literary quality of the presentation no doubt accounted for much of its success. But I also think that the superiority of the Collège de France as a free academic institution, a pure creation of Humanism, played a gracious part in the achievement. Despite the limited proportions of the building, its shabbiness and total lack of visual charm, the great foundation of the Renaissance presided, as it still presides, over the university life of France, because it has no ulterior purpose beyond scholarship, because it has nothing to do with production in any other sense, because in it the dissemination of knowledge and learning is entirely gratis and its teaching free from the shackles of an examination system.

The Collège de France seemed to have but one defect. Founded in 1530 by Francis I as the Collège Royal, a group of teachers of the new learning, it was unfortunately not provided with a special meeting place or *local*. The buildings in the rue des Écoles are comparatively modern, undistinguished in appearance, and inadequate in size, at least for special attractions. The misfortune for those who wished to hear Bergson was that its largest classroom was much too small for the purpose. And so I am reduced to admitting, after this digression, that I did not *hear* Bergson, but I *saw* him lecture to an audience that looked as if it would not care to have missed a word and would remember every syllable as easily as I now recall these visual details of a scene that has more than once been far better described.

*

* *

From the midst of these peregrinations I was sharply recalled to Aberystwyth, because the conditions of my scholarship insisted

upon residence during at least one of the two years of tenure. In what spare time my months of enforced residence left me, I occupied myself with dreams and devices for going to—of all places!—Oxford. A couple of efforts to gain a scholarship at one or other of the colleges met with repulse. But what contacts I made with representatives of the colleges in question were so pleasant as to stimulate afresh my desire and determination to carry out this somewhat Quixotic scheme. For after all, why should an amateur 'researcher' chasing the ghost of an 'influence' through the byeways of a modern literature insist upon choosing as field of operations the most staid and venerable of universities, and particularly (for such was his secret design) the most hard-headed and strenuous of her colleges? This was what the redoubtable W. P. Ker tartly insinuated when consulted upon my prospects. Of course it was folly—the divinest intrusion of fool-hardiness in the whole of my pusillanimous career! But behind this piece of audacity moved a benevolent providence. The slow machinery of Principal Roberts' solicitude had got quietly to work. By the middle of a new term it had ground a way for me through formidable difficulties and obstructions, and when the first autumn of the War was thinning the leaves and emptying the common rooms of Oxford, there was I with a room of my own in Balliol, and the prospect of a fellowship from my old college to keep me going.

CHAPTER EIGHT

PASTURES NEW

OUT of a dream, or perhaps from a remark overheard in childhood, or from a 'view' intercepted while turning the leaves of a picture-book, comes a persistent vision. A group of young men stand in easy attitudes on a sunlit lawn before a grave building. An ideal of enviable urbanity is realised in their unaffected grace and fellowship.

At Oxford I used to think I had found the scene of my premonition by looking through a gateway in Parks Road which everyone will know. My arrival, however, was a less visionary affair than this day-dream could have led me to expect. 'Tell him to come up at once, if he wants to come in,' ran a message received from the Master a fortnight after term had begun. Up I came in a flurry, flinging a luckless fare to the man who had offered to carry my bags from the taxi to my rooms. There I sat surveying the magnolia bush beside the dining hall staircase. Presently I heard a tap at the door. A short dignified figure entered. I rose hastily. 'Sir,' said the visitor in a tone that made me regret my impulse, 'the taxi-man's still at the lodge.'

'But I paid him ten minutes ago.'

'That wasn't him, sir.'

Life was full of such incongruities. One noon, as I walked out of College to look for lunch, the porter accosted me: 'Mr. Smith wishes to see you at once for matriculation. You'll want cap, gown and fees.' The cap and gown were being thrust upon me when someone in regalia swept round a corner and led me off to the Master's house. Our intrusion seemed to galvanise to unwonted activity an old gentleman we found waiting somnolently in a pleasant room. He began to mumble Latin phrases with pauses for responses which were filled by my energetic sponsor before I realized that he was metaphorically taking the words out of my mouth. Then the Master placed a volume of Statutes in my hands and Mr. Smith enquired whether I had any money. If not, he would lend me some.

With such precipitation I was rushed into membership of the University of Oxford. Still I was there at last, there by aspiration, condescension and luck, not by right of tradition, scholarship or any other right. Having no qualification to justify calling myself a Balliol man except through the grace of admission in wartime, I shall speak of the influence of the College and of Oxford as having been transmitted through imponderables, enriching with indirect benefits a mind ill-equipped but eagerly submissive. Such was not of course the specific kind of influence Balliol conveyed through her famous tutorials, but from them I was debarred by 'research' status. Yet my thoughts revert to the two years I spent there with constancy and gratitude for gifts that are difficult to describe except by the clichés commonly used for the effects the older universities are reputed to have on their alumni: the collegiate way of life, the serious attitude to learning, the blend of austerity and kindness that I found in the College that adopted me; the unemphatic distinction that stamped most things around people, manners, speech—and what struck a Welshman most strongly—the attitude of reserve and non-familiarity ingrained even in the unobsequious attentions of scouts and porters, and the general respect for the authorities; nor should I forget the spell exerted almost unconsciously by the older and finer buildings.

Of all my impressions of the time the one I prize most is that of the quality of the young men themselves or at least of those I met— by far the most serious group of *students* I had come across. The variety of individual minds and of national types, even in the depleted population of wartime, transmitted a sense of heterogeneous superiorities which were none the less unobtrusive. Undergraduates and graduates all appeared willing to think and to think for themselves. Not one of them but had a personal interest in reading. They were there to read history or the classics and to discuss freely what they had read, undistracted by any immediate pressure of an examination system. That word of ill omen, 'exams.,' so familiar in modern universities, seemed to have no equivalent in their jargon They might speak, when the time arrived, of 'schools,' and it was assumed that Balliol names would top most of the class-lists. But I cannot recall having heard the word 'examination' pronounced by an Oxford voice in my time. True, the strange word 'collections' was audible now and then; but it seemed to imply none of that

narrow confinement within a 'course', barricaded with terminal tests, such as had dominated the previous régime.

Then again the undergraduates had read with evident interest outside the subject that was their main objective and seemed ready to break a lance in discussion over a wide field of topics, many of which I had heard of only by name. Books they bought cautiously but of their own choice. (In Wales we were not without the wish but without the cash to indulge it.) And they would borrow books from one another for the pleasure of reading them, not merely for what they could get out of them for help with the course. From such men, most of them younger than myself, I felt I had much to learn and little to offer in return. If I contributed a jot to the reading of any of my contemporaries it was through lending an occasional borrower a cheap, ink-scored copy of *Leaves of Grass*.

This choice of text must not be taken as a sign of universal comradeship. A number of Americans and Colonials (very pleasant fellows) figured among my contemporaries. Not one of them approved of Whitman and the most moralistic reservations came from the fastest livers. For the authentic Balliol men introductions were *de rigueur*, after which you might not be perceived as you passed, although the quadrangle paths were scarcely wider than the staircases. In Wales you were friends at first sight; or thought you were. In the course of a stroll ('Going my way?' 'No, but I'll come.') you would learn most things of importance about your new acquaintance including the name of his birthplace: Tonypandy, Llanybyther, Splott. In Oxford I used to wonder who was the chap that had smiled in that other man's room and what the smile, if it was one, could have meant.

No attempt is being made here to describe life at Balliol during the first world war. I simply recall Jones at Balliol, a lean, malingering figure of a man who seemed to think it worthwhile doing something with or on French literature. (He was intercepted in the College library reading that incurable ranter, Victor Hugo.) Yet how could two consecutive years spent in the College have been other than a precious part of life's experience, even for a person confined to such limited means of contact as were mine? With these reservations I feel I may risk a few more impressions.

Balliol in wartime, though depleted in numbers, looked anything but a close-knit society. Between undergraduates studying different

subjects or belonging to different years intercommunication was not easy: such a diversity of wits and temperaments reigned as to preclude unanimity, to say nothing of *esprit de corps*. Yet if cliques were discernible they were not obtrusive. I came to know relatively few men even of my year of entry, but I was not conscious of ostracism beyond the exclusion imposed by my rare and odd type of subject.

The objectivity of so much of the life and talk fascinated me. Among the best people the modes of speech were simple, rarely over-subtle or sophisticated. No topic was over-elaborated. One could not help noticing how few words were used and how they would be chosen: as simple as possible provided they conveyed the sense, but with the emphasis on the word that confirmed the meaning. Slang, colloquial facilities or vapid abstractions that might dilute or divert its force were evaded. It was fascinating to watch this avoidance of clichés. One hadn't realized how many spontaneous observations are really quite unnecessary! There could be horrifying gaps without them. But what a reward after abysms of silence to hear English spoken! Or to wander through quadrangles when they filled with shadows and the lamps were lit in the high rooms, the softest voices on earth floating down with a little music—never very much or too professionally played—thinly floating through the trees.

Of course there were snobberies. Those you knew might be several, but those who knew you were very few. The rest had a way of looking *near* you and doubtless *through* you, but never *at* you. So that you could neither nod nor smile in reply. Had you waved a hand or handkerchief to draw their gaze over that infinitesimal interstice between their line of vision and your own, you could not tell whether they would be infuriated or scared. Anything might ensue, from a snub to an assault.

A certain degree of stiffness or of distance seemed commendable, based no doubt on a sensitive respect for individual autonomy. Reserve was dominant; but what tentative breaches were made through the shield could be ingratiating: the reserve of one individual assuming that of the other. Nothing here of that easy familiarity pervading the entire college society one had found in Wales and warmly appreciated when first one came upon it. Nor of that noisy element that could disrupt and tyrannize to no purpose.

Here genuine idiosyncrasy was free to flourish even at the expense of companionship. Yet such associations as were formed were all the more sincere for being discreet; they might blossom into life-long friendships.

There is, however, a freak of behaviour or a studied attitude which has for me been one of the minor puzzles of personality. It belongs strictly to certain persons who are obviously in possession of gifts which someone of my type would feel no kind of embarrassment in acknowledging as superior to any of his own, and yet who exhibit a conspicuous apathy towards those whom they find less talented or less advantaged than themselves. This kind of *hauteur* was not frequently displayed during my two years' residence, perhaps because so few of those left were of pure stock. Now and then only could one detect a sign of *outrecuidance* that seemed incompatible with the *effortless* superiority a Balliol prime minister was soon to declare to the world as the mark of the College alumnus.

For relief my memory turns to evoke a short, thick-set, square-headed man, roughly garbed, almost unkempt, with full lips and remarkably deep brown eyes, burnished and smouldering like peat fires in a swarthy face under close-cropped, upright hair. You might have passed him by without a glance but for the sound of his voice—the purest accent of a distinctive culture—and that dark steadfast gaze. They belonged to a man whose type of brain was afterwards compared with Churchill's, fated to die young, but not without having illustrated the name of Jan Hendrich Hofmeyr.

My friends? Dreamlike they return and what charm they had! R. D. Roberts and Gover both doing medicine; tall and serious J. D. I. Hughes, who, with E. T. John, read law. Eager, not excitable talkers, they shared the art of blending humour with argument. Their frequent exchange of mufti for khaki brought us back to the horrors of the time. The holocausts were on. Beyond Worcester gardens the hospital trains moved slowly in, the engine of one train close to the rear of another, filled with wounded and dying men.

News came one day that John had been killed—not before the rest of us had recognized in him a quiet man of delicate perceptions, one of the gentlest natures we had met. The rare quality of masculine charm without effeminacy I should not have known otherwise.

A few others there were whom I knew less well. I see their

attitudes and hear their voices blend in tones of genial seriousness indicating their balance of mind. Among them a few Americans and Australians, well nurtured, handsome men, ready to interpose with a gust of free philosophy, when too much sophistication needed a breath of air. The Snell scholar of the year would drop into a group, a bottle of scotch protruding from his pocket. When it was empty he might mistake your bedroom for his and retreat with fervent, if faltering, apologies. And there were more critical minds beyond the reach of my acquaintance, who might be heard propounding views of staggering boldness. 'Love,' one of the wits asserted, 'was sex plus imagination . . .' One Sunday morning our good friend, Gover, had led an attack on the Disciples for letting down the Master. That evening, swept in by a group entering another man's room, I found half the company gathered before a sofa where an elongated figure, that of Aldous Huxley, his head and feet protruding beyond the ends of the couch, was visibly struggling— the Milton word, 'convolved', came incongruously into my mind— with the problem of what God was.

And there were feats of valor and the reverse.

No one of my year was more popular than C. M. Macinnes. Smitten in boyhood with a fever that had deprived him of sight, he would move unerringly to the seat he had occupied when first he sat in one's room, referring to objects around as if he could see them clearly. It was hard to disbelieve the tallest story of his exploits when you had gauged the degree of physical strength condensed in his short but upright frame. Taking a couple of ladies out in a canoe, he had dashed under a bough which caught their large hats and over-turned the craft. Rescuing both and placing them safely on the bank, he had plunged back for the canoe and secured that too.

However much truth there was behind this story, a clumsy intervention of mine on the Cherwell came near to a worse disaster. Half a dozen Welshmen had taken a punt out and, the day being warm, had found shelter under a willow near Parson's Pleasure. After a spell one of the company, Clifford Jones, a pleasant, good-looking man, took up the pole to push off from the bank. Finding we had got stuck, he called a time or two for help. Stretched on the cushions in the bottom of the craft, I applied my feet to the overhanging trunk and pressed hard. Out swung the stern of the

punt in a swift semi-circle and Cliff disappeared. Before we realised what had happened he came to the surface, beads of water streaming from his jet-black hair and a cry on his lips which made us roar with amusement and relief: 'Oh, my best presentation watch!'

We hauled him in, and there he sat, indifferent to his condition, without a word of reproach, contemplating a gold watch with a speck of water on its face. This was one of our last meetings. He too was killed at the front shortly afterwards.

It would be an impertinence to recommend the life of a College whose characteristic activities and strengths I knew mainly by observation and report. The memory of that life—or should I not say of its external aspects?—recalls none the less a phase I am most grateful not to have missed. It was a mode of the life of scholarship: selective, conditioned and reserved, but devoted, ideally at least, to serious attitudes of mind and to the study of grave and high things, which increase in numbers now threatens to debilitate and degrade. What did I see last summer when walking round the inner quadrangle? Empty bottles discarded on the lawn . . .

But what, let us retort, was that odd man Jones—the only one of his name in College in 1914—doing beside observing the life around and reading yellow-backs?

My admission, I assume, was a trifle incongruous. Usually the College expected its undergraduates to read for Honours. But war had been declared, prospective Honours candidates were scarce and the rule or custom had been relaxed. I was one of a few research entries, but in an unusual subject. A scene enacted before term was well advanced puts the modest eccentricity of my situation in a somewhat amusing light.

One evening the venerable Scotsman who was still Master during my first year gave a periodic dinner-party, to which I was invited. Our host was notoriously shy in company, with that delicious mixture of simplicity, deference and aversion to conversation or easy sociability which is or was the British ideal of a scholar's deportment. The Master's timidity seemed to infect most of us as we took up consciously nonchalant attitudes along the walls of the spacious reception room. With drowsy courtesy the bowed figure passed from one laconic guest to another, handing each a small

card inscribed with his place at table, and trying to make a few appropriate remarks. Only the Master's cat seemed at ease in the company, striding casually across the carpet from one zone of apprehension to another. As the sleek monster approached, each man leapt in spirit upon this providential topic and strove to invent something less banal than the previous futility. I was one of a small group who were anxiously discussing the cat when the Master reached us. Having acknowledged the others he turned a troubled gaze in my direction. Hesitating as if to make sure that my unique surname applied to the wavering figure before him, he murmured with the maximum of embarrassment: 'Oh, Jones . . . you are . . . let me see . . . you are, I believe, the . . . the . . . *natural science* man, aren't you?'

A movement of friendly concern passed through our little group as with an effort I confessed I was doing French. 'Ah yes!', he said, 'I knew it was one of those out of the way . . .' If playfulness was intended, it was evidently felt to have gone too far, and out of deference, perhaps, to my feelings an awkward silence supervened. Suddenly a voice piped up beside me: 'He's doing Verhaeren, you know, Master.' 'Verhaeren? . . . Verhaeren? . . .' The tones grew angelically distant. Then they descended to earth: 'Isn't *Raemakers* a wonderful man!'

The meal was even more frigid than the reception. We ate in silence but for one audacious voice that persisted in describing a funicular: 'And it went up and up and up.' The speaker lent back from the table and inscribed rings of sublime ascent with his forefinger. Huxley could never have had a more clinging audience.

Nothing would be more alien to the spirit of the College than to apply pretentious terms or inappropriate titles to its senior members. I shall therefore not use the phrase 'moral tutor' of the Fellow to whom I was appointed to report. Nor would 'supervisor' fit, having precisely an alien sound. The word 'mentor' had carried the fame of a previous Master of Balliol to the four corners of the learned world. But Mr. F. F. Urquart could hardly be designated by so intimate a term in relation to myself. I had no occasion to call on him frequently, although my rare consultations remain memorable for me. The steel-grey hair, the puckered brow and the distant kindly manner are unforgettable. So is their wartime setting: the long room with the many photos of his friends and pupils in

khaki arranged round the walls. It was Mr. Urquart who prompted one of the most momentous decisions of my academic youth. But before coming to that I must relate how he gave me a word of encouraging reproof.

To assure him I was doing some work I passed on an offprint of an article that had just appeared in the *Modern Language Review*. My exercise was contrived in obedience to the dominant method of the time in *comparatiste* studies. It kept strictly to the facts of the case and presented them with trite concision. Mr. Urquart returned the exercise at the foot of his staircase with the remark: 'D'you know, Jones, I think an essay on literature should open windows on the infinite.' The observation may sound slight and off-hand. But what relief it brought ultimately to a temperament cramped by the narrowness of the techniques I was involved in then and for long after! Academically it paid to spot the *petite bête* and not to look out of the window.

Before my first term was over the question arose of a choice of subject to work on for the B.Litt. degree. The extent to which I had been attracted by the poetry of Verhaeren has sufficiently been indicated. To write a book in English on him seemed the ideal job. But not for a moment did I anticipate that such a venture would be acceptable to the Oxford authorities. This is how the momentous decision was made.

What was I going to do? Mr. Urquart asked.

'Something on Verhaeren.'

'Why not write a book on him?'

'But', I queried, 'would the Univeristy take it for a thesis?'

'We'll see', he said.

No one supervised my studies. I read a little in the Bodleian, in the Camera, in the Taylorian, in my rooms. My difficulty was to get sufficiently recent publications. This was not, I admit, in the manner of the College to which I was admitted. One morning seated on the lawn under the trees, I was turning over the pages of a yellow-back when Mr. A. L. Smith dashed past. Catching sight of the covers he turned abruptly and shouted: 'Rotten stuff, isn't it?' He might have been less incensed had he known it was Jules Romains' *L'Ame de la Ville*.

Yet there was actually a tutor in modern languages attached to the College . . .

More than once Mr. Urquart had enquired had I seen Mr.
Bourdillon. The name was familiar as that of the author of an
edition of *Aucassin et Nicolette*, that exquisite *chantfable* we had
laboriously deflowered in our Welsh Honours course. But that was
Bourdillon *père*. Now I was to discover the euphonious name
painted on a lintel in a far corner of the inner quad. Keeping a
look-out I noticed now and then a slightly senior figure disappearing
up the distant staircase to reappear very quickly and vanish.
Prompted by this rare apparition I wrote, and received an invitation
to visit Mr. Bourdillon, not in College, but at his country home, a
ten-mile journey away. The scene as I recall it was idyllic: a small
farm, modest and natural in fact, but idealized in my mind by the
perfection of its details compared with the sombreness of my life,
harassed with malady. Mrs. Bourdillon and her small children
were models of robust health and the white sheep, the spotless pigs
and placid cows had a kind of clean rotundity, much like figures in
the paintings of Sir Stanley Spencer. After tea we lay in the hay
and Mr. Bourdillon asked the question that had become customary
by now: what was I doing? Under the spell of my harmonious
surroundings I embarked on a cautious account of Verhaeren's
work, emphasizing the 'uplift' in the benevolent collections of his
maturity. This didn't seem to interest my hearer. 'Wasn't there
something different?' he asked. I plunged into the turgidities of
Les Soirs, Les Débâcles, Les Flambeaux noirs. My host relaxed:
the wide-eyed children and the perfect domestic animals gathered
round and all seemed well until a sharp whistle announced the
train that was to take me back to Oxford. I had seen Mr. Bourdillon.

Things were not always so easy. My readiness to respect superior
judgements got a jolt one evening when I read a paper on Verhaeren's
poetry to a literary group in College. The earliest of his many
collections, *Les Flamandes*, had scandalized the *bien pensants* when
it appeared in 1883. But its crude pastiches of Rubens, Jordaens
and Teniers played only a preliminary role in the general orchestra-
tion of his *œuvre*.

The first man who spoke after my paper announced: 'I don't like
fat women.' This was a body-blow. It knocked Jones out.

Another time Sir Walter Raleigh allowed me to have a talk with
him in Magdalen Hall after a morning lecture. He was gracious and
attentive until I told him I had met Verhaeren in Paris. Then he

reacted, warning me that personal acquaintance might damage judgement. Perhaps it did. Some years later Madame Verhaeren told me they had never met so enthusiastic an Englishman as myself. I hope this admission will appear more naïve than fatuous. It goes far to explain a faintly critical attitude to Jones in Balliol.

One day, to the mild surprise of my scout, a young woman with handsome features and jet black hair burst into my room and announced that she intended to bring round a friend who was setting the Academy of Music alight with her gifts and prospects. Elizabeth Lloyd, a distinguished Aberystwyth graduate, had come up to consult manuscripts in the Bodleian about the history of the Eisteddfod. When next she came, after familiar greetings Elizabeth stepped aside and one of the few apparitions I have met in life confronted me. A shy, enigmatic little person stood watching me with dark, quizzical eyes. Confusedly I wondered was she a child, a girl or a fairy. It was clear that her small person was suffused with sensibility. She approached gently; there was laughter with a touch of mockery in her gaze. This was my first glimpse of Morfudd Owen, the capricious, ill-fated young singer and composer of whom the Head of the Academy was reported to have said in an aside: 'You see that little monkey over there? Well, that little devil could do anything.'

Morfudd returned to Oxford a few times and met some of my friends who seemed as much fascinated and mystified by her eccentricities as I was. One of her foibles was to wear vast round hats whose diameters must have measured half her own height. Under these awnings mercurial changes could sweep her moods. She would indulge in the gamineries of a child, breaking into un-controllable fits of laughter or of tears at the slightest provocation. Like so many young Welsh people Morfudd loved to make light of the proprieties and to mock the hierarchies whenever a chance occurred. In London one evening she and Elizabeth had been taken out to dinner by a couple of men attached to a ministry. The party had passed off well and, taxis being scarce in wartime, the men decided to take their guests home by tube. Before entering the lift one of the girls remembered they were short of bread in the flat they shared and, after a long search, a loaf was found by one of

their escort. Being in high spirits Morfudd stuck the loaf on the tip of her *en tout cas* and, to the embarrassment of the other passengers, she marched round the lift holding the bread in the air. Then feeling she had disgraced Elizabeth in the presence of their new acquaintances, she lowered the trophy and sobbed on her friend's shoulder for the rest of the journey.

Not long after these incidents Morfudd was married to Dr. Ernest Jones, the psycho-analyst, to whom with a few friends I was subsequently introduced. The following autumn I was staying as a guest at the home-farm of Singleton Abbey, where Dr. and Mrs. Denzil Harries were holding a house-party. One afternoon Dr. Ernest Jones called bringing the dreadful news of his wife's death in hospital as the result of an unsuitable anaesthetic. I accompanied Dr. Jones back to his home in Oystermouth. A few words were exchanged. I had not realized till then with what force the blankness of death in youth can strike a man of feeling.

It is out of the fashion to sing the praises of Oxford. For that, if for no other reason, this account of my experiences will hardly be arresting. Try as I may, I can find nothing evil to say of the place as I knew it at a period which, since it coincided with the first two years of the War, cannot, I am aware, be claimed as typical. It was a 'select' Oxford, perhaps, that recommended itself cunningly enough to my alien taste. Alien, because Oxford requires a long and special incubation. Her spirit must attend the schooling or early preparation of her future alumnus. It must haunt his home. Only a nucleus of undergraduates can have received this initiation, but it is they who make Oxford. I do not mean that it is only they who can appreciate the place or profit by a sojourn there.

Without any partiality of which I am aware I have always considered my two years at Balliol as the most valuable part of my (ir)regular education. It was the only time when I felt definitely brought up against standards; the first time, I mean, when I was in contact with people and things that I felt to be genuinely superior. And this does not refer mainly to those whom I found above me in official positions. During the whole of my time in College I never crossed the threshold of a lecture room, and I had no more than half-a-dozen consultations about my work or destiny. Yet

I was tolerated, I was secretly pampered within, though never far within, the pale of this austere academy, to whose prestige I contributed less, far less, than the genial scout who was so attentive to my daily needs;* or the Bursar's clerk who as he intoned my surname when battels were presented before the Master in hall could little have guessed the thrill it gave me to rise for once a man and not a multitude. Apart from health I lived a life of tranquility, unruffled by impositions or interferences of any kind. My few brief contacts with the dons were agreeable incidents. Their kindness, their manners were pleasant enough in an unemphatic way to fill one with regret that opportunities for meeting them were so rare. Illusory occasions of ideal relationships, perhaps; naïve impressions, no doubt, which would have suffered modification had meetings been frequent or relations more sustained. Oxford remains one of the few dreams realized in life because, it may be, the dreamer never woke up.

While it imparted a sense of standards and values never hitherto realized, Balliol, thanks no doubt to my somewhat anomalous position there, did little or nothing to ease my difficulties as to expression. How often have I regretted that we 'researchers' were considered either too insignificant or too experienced to be asked to write essays according to the weekly custom of the College that harboured us. The day of retribution was thus put off. In the end it came like the biblical thief, though not without making amends.

I do not claim that better progress would have been made with my earlier phase of training were it bereft of the aids and contacts, the control and supervision of modern academic routine. I cannot help being grateful, however, for the immense relief felt in passing from a milieu where everything connected with one's work was kept prominently before one by the recurrent pressure of courses, classes, lectures, exercises and examinations with the atmosphere of compulsion, competition and apprehension they produce. When subsequently one became conscious of the higher values of the new régime, the lesson was appreciated and its point unforgettably driven home. It would be grossly incorrect, of course, to give the

---

* At one low ebb Adams was instructed to bring breakfast to my room—as often as not lamb chops fried in breadcrumbs. In contrast, war-time lunch in hall consisted of rolls, butter, cheese and water. Why does each item of this diet still seem delicious on the tongue despite my feckless digestion?

impression that all the people around one at Oxford were indifferent to prescribed work. Few of them but had their quota of academic trials to face. The difference was that they did not talk about them with the respect or the antipathy to which I had been accustomed. Rarely, if ever, did I hear 'results' mentioned, except in jest, even by people whom I knew to be taking these things seriously. I am anxious, however, not to leave the impression that I think modern universities could or should model themselves on the older type. I merely hint that the youngest of them, when they have fulfilled the obvious functions for which they were designed, should look to Oxford to soften their asperities rather than follow the Metropolis in keeping them sharp.

I am still inclined to discover the secret of Oxford where Newman found it. One's contemporaries, the companions with whom one was in daily touch, were one's educators. Here was a society from which one had something—an enormous amount—to learn through contacts, conversations and the observation of manners and modes of life and thought. Admiration, uncritical no doubt, if not excessive, for most of what I was surrounded by, along with a readiness to recognize my own relative deficiencies, made for a peaceful, rapid and stimulating assimilation through natural curiosity and a tendency to compare, which was at times almost unconscious, at times perhaps only too consciously felt.

It was through some of my associates that I began to realize for myself something of the meaning of the words, 'art' and 'expression', and to gain a sense of quality, standard and taste in these spheres. One morning a person whom I still think of with gratitude and respect gave me the fine surprise of calling unannounced at my rooms. We were soon plunged in unembarrassed conversation which was for me of the most exciting kind. I had never been on speaking terms with anyone who gave me nearly the same sense of mastery and penetration in critical acumen. Across a flight of years that friendly 'interview' remains vivid and intact, dominated by an aquiline visage and quizzical eyes that seemed to gauge with kindly clairvoyance the slender stock of my knowledge and the limits of my experience. It was part of the strange, complex thrill of under-graduate interdiscovery. Nothing comparable could happen again.

This visit was a propitious event. It gave unhoped for access to the literary group that reigned at that moment under the ascendancy

of T. W. Earp and which, for all its vanity, did not flourish in vain, at least not quite in vain for me.

When next Earp called he found me in another room on a recent staircase whose lattice windows admitted more light. Three small pictures I had hastily begged my father to send up from his stock of odds and ends could thus be seen more clearly. One was an old print of an English sea-captain in knee-breeches and three-cornered hat, picked out in a few bright colours. Earp scrutinized this carefully. Then turning to me with a slightly raised eyebrow he murmured: 'An ancestor?'

CHAPTER NINE

THE DOWNFALL OF JONES

IN response to the invitation from Earp I mount the stairs of his lodgings to the large sitting-room on the first landing. From that distant day to this the noble street with its smooth façades and fine iron balconies means for me, as it corners with John Street, Earp's Coterie.

My first visit filled me with dismay. The atmosphere seemed thick with affectations. Hypersensitive superciliousness waited upon nervous suspicion. Anything more incredibly *manqué*—not frigid but feverish with suspense and paralysed by the appalling risks of utterance—I could not have imagined. Sounds and sights were subdued as in a seance where voices murmur laconically with dreamy apologetic tremors. The few devotees who broke silence seemed to be uttering drivel. The nasal timbre of a tenacious American reading a rudimentary sonnet sequence struck an amazing, a scarcely reassuring anti-climax. It seemed a voice from earth. The reader's manner is assured, confident, unperturbed by the silence into which, one after another, his compositions drop. The other members are more and more embarrassed but not the sonneteer who has always another up his sleeve to be detached from the series and read aloud with echoless aplomb. Our host sits behind inscrutable, motionless save for an occasional twitch of the eyebrows, an impersonal habit marvellous to intercept, but which augurs no approval. This sort of reception for the reader injures my generous Welsh soul. Not courageous enough to protest I cannot suppress a murmur or two of resentment. My murmurs fall unheeded into the circumambient stillness. Before long I quit the room with no desire to return.

I did return, and while I remained in Oxford rarely missed a meeting. I began to feel my way about those silences. A strain of artistic sincerity underlay all this mummery, at least in the best of the group. I soon became aware that some of its members had accomplishments far superior to any I had met with hitherto. An incomparable stock of literary knowledge, an acute acquaintance with detail, allied with a subtlety in discrimination which were

deceptive to a newcomer of my doric breeding simply because they were worn lightly with indifferent or ironic ease. My sensitiveness—or my insensitiveness—to affectation and mannerism was soon inoculated with a proper recognition of virtues under the mask which scared me with salutary effect. I could hear myself, when I ventured to speak, mouthing commonplaces of text-book orthodoxy. My experiments in studied pentameters began to wear an apologetic, not to say a wistful, air. The scantiness of my knowledge in general, the uncertainty of my grasp of the things I thought I knew, the insecurity of what standards I posessed, above all a disquieting feeling of the futility of such efforts as I had made to think and to write came home to me gradually, without too much alarm.

I shall be laughed at for assimilating Coterie to a school of poetry. But I insist. What it 'taught' me was the importance of *préciosité*. There are epochs when the appropriate and inevitable mode of expression is a form of preciousness. That affected by the aspirants of 1915 made my Victorian rhetoric sound empty and unprofitable. And I was soon persuaded of the folly of dissipating a slender energy in pursuing a line along which one could not hope to catch up with the tail of one's contemporaries.

It became apparent that, costive as the discussions were, timorous or inconclusive, producing no argument, defence or debate, one or two of the more regular members and two or three who dropped in occasionally were worth hearing when they read a piece of verse. And Earp himself was always worth watching even when he didn't read, so much was effected by a shrug, a grimace, an air of blank indifference. The impersonal mask might now and then frown with disapproval or cautiously flicker with faint commendation: 'That has come off . . . I think . . . yes, *just.*' The very last thing his group could have been called was a school of flattery. Gradually emerged a respect for the master and a perception of critical distinctions very much finer than I had derived from any of the 'masters' I had heard or seen hitherto. Before long I had the feeling that the leader of Coterie had summed me up but did not wish me to leave. Not even after the day of my downfall.

How far I was justified in this estimate of things, judged from my present standpoint, is a question which does not interest me much at this juncture. I am concerned only to indicate the reaction of the milieux I passed through in each phase of my development at

the moment of incidence. It is true that the description or analysis of each 'incidence' is related to the present through memory. But memory has recalled these experiences time after time since the events, and I cannot perceive that there has been much change in my estimate of the facts thus re-presented.

Retrospect may nonetheless play an unconscious role in accentuating inferiorities that were not acknowledged or recognized at the time. Let it be granted that a maturer sense of personal defects and of deficiencies in one's training has coloured the past. What I was unmistakably aware of at Oxford, along with a sense of vagueness and inchoateness in myself, was a revulsion from that *inaccuracy* of thought and expression which my previous training had done less to correct than to facilitate. It was a curious shock to find the Oxford man so hard-headed, so informed of detail, so exact, so exacting under the languid manner. Only one tender and how refreshing duperie could I detect—a juvenile faith in the ubiquitous blossoming of genius.

Among the most faithful members of the group during the terms I attended were Wilfred Childe and Eric Dickinson. Childe with his short nose and innocent blue eyes, and a touch of yellow contrived in his green shirt collar, was the most picturesque of us. He intimated to me how much like Keats Dickinson looked and, as a compliment to my wretched health, I'll admit he compared my lean profile to Dante's. Russell Green came frequently and read verses, and occasionally Huxley would appear and amaze us with the brilliance and *élan* of poems soon to be collected in *The Burning Wheel*.

Earp was obviously pleased when both or either of those gifted Irishmen, E. R. Dodds and L. A. G. Strong, looked in. Strong, whom I heard reading on a few occasions, left an attractive impression of Earp and the Coterie in his unfinished autobiography. One afternoon, I clearly recall, Robert Nichols turned up in khaki and disturbed the balance by leaning on the mantelpiece and declaiming a set of harrowing impressions of life and death in the trenches. He had just returned from the front and read with dramatic intensity in a voice trembling with emotion. I suspect most of us were moved to the point of resentment. 'That kind of thing isn't art,' Earp was heard to protest next day.

What degree of impropriety he was willing to admit could be

gauged from another special occasion—the afternoon appointed
for the reception of two Oxford women poets, Miss Dorothy
Sayers and Miss Elizabeth Rendall who, it was surreptitiously
arranged, should attend Coterie unaccompanied by a chaperon.
Minors like myself came in force. Nor could we resist envying the
nonchalance with which the ladies read their compositions without
apologetic coughs or furtive glances at the master who with restrained
courtesy seemed almost to approve of their aplomb.

Disposed by nature to a rigorous art, Earp as a critic was in
reaction from the loose facilities indulged in by the contemporary
tiros of the *vers libre*. To give an example in restraint he had already
published *Chisellings*, his own strict experiments in rhymeless
verse.* All my own longings for the North Midlands are packed
into:

> "Notts,"
>   You said.
> And I said,
> "Notts—
> Oh yes,
> Of course,
> But there are other places."
>
> And then I was silent quickly,
> For I remembered certain fields
> Where I played when I was a child,
> With the November sunset over them.

His reactions against Georgian facilities were, I should now say,
somewhat like Ezra Pound's. But I must be careful not to imply
that either Earp's ideas or his experiments owed anything to Pound,
of whose contemporary demonstrations he did not appear to
approve.

It is probable that what Earp thought of as models were Arthur
Waley's translations from Chinese and Japanese originals. The
Noh plays, for instance, I remember having heard him refer to with
admiration. Earp was a strict but courteous critic, liable to meet
self-approval in others with silence or an ironic sally. Yet he gave
no offence. Those who felt the flick of his lash liked him none the less.

It will have been assumed that he played the major role as host
to the group. Occasionally the rendez-vous shifted and once at

* Collected in *Contacts*.

least it came round to me. It is a relief to think I had not a pocketful
of sonnets to dispose of with tea and iced cake from Balliol 'shop'.
All I could muster were a few translations, most of them from
Verhaeren. I began with a sonnet whose lightning-struck gloom had
always fascinated me:

> Par les plaines de ma crainte, tournée au Nord,
> Voici le vieux berger des Novembres qui corne,
> Debout, comme un malheur, au seuil du bercail morne,
> Qui corne au loin l'appel des troupeaux de la mort . . .

At the seventh line of my rendering a cultured voice broke in:
viorne wasn't 'verbena'! On some previous occasion I had thrust
a word in that I knew for one I had no time to look up. My
ignorance had to be confessed and I floundered through the
remainder. The silence that followed was broken by the lofty
voice suggesting a round-robin. Someone other than Earp had
taken over that evening, though Earp was present. Silence returned
while we scribbled our couplets. They were gathered up and read
out by the peremptory young genius who had seized the initiative.
An ominous line ending with 'dead bones' brought round the rhyme,

> . . . damn Jones!

Would it had stopped there! How proud I should be to declare
which of the gods had damned me this time! But the next line swept
the rest of the company by their names into perdition—all except
three. Earp, Childe and the speaker* escaped the doom. What
better example could there be of the inscrutable workings of
Predestination? The elect were safe.

Earp would never have indulged in such direct exposure. But
his disapproval could be firm. The point of his objection would
come at the end of a demonstration, rarely at the beginning; his
reproof might be definite but never sustained. There was nothing
of the schoolmaster about him.

Earp's kindness to me did not relax after this exposure. Nor did
my curmudgeon persistence stop practising Boileau's wretched
injunction to those who lack gift:

> Polissez-le sans cesse et le repolissez . . .

---

* It was Aldous Huxley.

At last a few years' grind on an impression of elm-trees was licked into alliterative sonnet-form and cautiously read to Childe. Wilfred, whom I saw more frequently than any of the others, appeared to like it. A few days later Earp dropped in and asked could he hear the sonnet. He wore, I well remember, light grey tweeds with a crimson handkerchief protruding from the chest pocket. Before I had read a few lines he slumped delicately in the chair and waved the crimson silk as if to ward off too luscious an odour. Some time later he asked me for a copy to print, adding surreptitiously: 'You like the line . . .'

It was in watching men like Earp and Childe at work that the salutary realization grew upon me of the *literalness* of my mind. This didn't depress me too much. Ill-health was still a major encumbrance absorbing all other forms of discouragement or depression. I had long ago faced the limits of my intelligence and the slowness of its reactions. Whether a tortoise ever gets there first or not—and I think sometimes it does—what is not doubtful is that a tortoise takes more time to discover it is on the wrong path. What saved so many of my generation from continuing to clang the doleful lyre was the appearance of *The Waste Land*. If that was poetry we felt we had better dry up. Forty years have elapsed. *The Waste Land* is poetry.

Earp's Coterie was in its limited, resistant way an empire within an empire. It was by no means without laws and customs for having no written constitution; its tone was anything but free and easy, and it was autonomous. Coterie had no kind of connection with English studies in the University, although it could hardly have been what it was at that period, were it not composed mainly of undergraduates in one of the older universities. Of lecturers, professors or tutors I can recall not even a mention, except that Earp himself had a clear respect for Sir Walter Raleigh and a sensitive regard for good scholarship. Examinations were caricatured in the recurrent farce of Earp's presenting himself for 'divvers' at such times as he remembered to turn up. A new pipe perceived in a tobacconist's window was enough to deflect his purpose.

Viewing in retrospect this small group and its leaders, what seems remarkable is the absolute purity of its aims. Its members were engaged on interests they found real for their own sakes: the writing and reading aloud of verse, punctuated by brief observations—

usually reservations—on its demerits. No hint of mercenary interests, not even of publishing, stole a moment's consideration from the cult of verse. Success meant 'bringing off' a poem, a verse, a line. 'It succeeds, I think', 'it comes off' were words of high praise. The master never taught by precept. He was strictly loyal to his ideal of what would do; and this ruled out a number of things you might have thought you had done pretty well. Writing decent verse, poetry if possible, was the objective. Nothing else mattered. The university, the war, the world might not have existed. All that happened of interest to the group happened in the private room of the singular man who was our host. Even to call his Coterie a form of gratuitous tutoring would debase it, so much was accomplished by silence.

I have no reason to believe that Earp, had he lived, would have approved of my writing him up. On the contrary I recall his reproving me for making a note in his presence. It is no excuse to add that all my memories of him are favourable. Here, however, I am telling my own story and Earp, as I saw him at Oxford, was an impressive exemplar. Never before had I seen standards of taste applied by a far abler man than myself. He and his peers concentrated on specimens actually produced in the milieu; and they judged them good or bad without brutal denunciation of the bad but without pretending that what was feeble was good enough. Not until *Scrutiny* appeared was I to see anything of the kind done again, but then, of course, much more explicitly and with objective examples drawn from widely accredited and discredited sources.

Of Coterie habitués Wilfred Childe was the only one who could be called picturesque, though none was less inclined to pose. For me he was a genuine *naif*, the first and the last I have ever met in academic milieux. An early collection of his, *The Little Cities*, anticipated my discovery of the Cotswold villages and their churches. *The Escaped Princess* appeared before I left Oxford and was passed on to me to notice for the *Isis*.

When I think of the interest I derived from attending Coterie meetings and ask myself what my contribution was, I cling to a dubious spar. I had once shown Earp a rough notebook in which he found, assiduously reproduced, the outlines of the famous little Symbolist review, *La Vogue*. Having placed the precious copy (lent me by the critic, Tancréde de Visan) flat on the page, I had

drawn lines round its periphery. A short time after this Earp produced the first number of the *Palatine Review*. I flatter myself (without proof) that my measurements and description had suggested the size and colour of the *Palatine*. How many literary influences have been founded on evidence as slight!*

T. W. Earp was one of the most distinctive personalities with whom I have ever been on terms that might be called friendly: our relations were at no time intimate. With more assurance I consider him the most influential of all undergraduates whom I met in my student days, although it might be difficult to point to any sign of his influence except the wise, restrictive effect he exerted unconsciously upon my one-time laborious efforts to write verse. In this way he exercised a refining restraint on my impulses, quite out of proportion to his intentions and to the brief period I spent in his neighbourhood. Looking back I perceive that what really impressed me I might call the spectacle of taste in action, even though it was Earp's *attitude* rather than his rare explicit judgements that counted most with me. When I think of a certain type of intellectual sensibility, acute, ironic, yet capable of deep feeling, I revert in memory to Earp in the belief that he belonged to that limited category for whom aesthetic values are the supreme, perhaps the unique, interests that poetry and the other arts inspire. It will be concluded that I have not spent much time in the company of creative writers: scholars, even literary scholars, have as a rule quite different temperaments.

Not that Earp corresponded to the effeminate type of pure aesthete. When I knew him a strong masculinity marked his attitudes and judgements. There was nothing 'pinky-dinky' about him. On the contrary, a robust element in his mind and personality kept his observations astringent. Perhaps it was a north-country strain that one seems to see developed in his portrait by Augustus John—an almost Teutonic cast of head and expression with a touch of *embonpoint*, of truculence, almost of grossness I had never perceived in the flesh, but with a faint suggestion of that *robustesse* of temperament, that jollity that could reassert itself at

---

* It should perhaps be added that in one number of the *Palatine* I reviewed some translations of books by Verhaeren. This gained the friendly attention of Michael Sadleir. A much larger publication called *Coterie* began to appear just after I had gone down. To one number of this review I contributed a prose impression of a beggar caught in the cold in Bloomsbury.

any time. What mannerisms he had were part of the man. A quick contraction of the eyebrows, a genuine *tic*, passed now and then over his rather saturnine mask: otherwise his movements were unexcited, usually a little slow. The face, as I remember it, was striking but in an unassuming, meditative way, in general shape aquiline, the profile *très fin*. The only eccentricity was his strange, cultured, sepulchral voice and unhurried but pointed speech. Of volubility not a trace. Restraint and the absence of clichés enabled the unobtrusive but unmistakable quality of the personality and its expressiveness to emerge. The unfailing but not emphatic courtesy, perhaps his most endearing trait, never standoffish but strictly without familiarity—distancing but not lacking in geniality—made up a personality totally unaffected but very special, not without stiffness but without pose, alluring to recall, for me quite unforgettable.

Sometimes a touch of fantasy crossed his mind. One morning he confided to me that, during a thunderstorm the previous midnight he had seen what Mallarmé meant in the flashes of lightening . . . I recall him, not as a specimen of the 'undergraduate', but as a true if capricious *student*, living, reading and thinking entirely outside the examination system, yet whose understanding of literature seemed far more mature than that of any examinee I had come across. At fifty years' distance I still think of him as one of the few really fascinating personalities I met in early life—'intriguing' in the full sense of the French word. In my very limited experience of literary types I should have to describe Earp as unique.

CHAPTER TEN

THE LAST ENCHANTMENT

ALORS, quoi—Il y a quelqu'un qui se moque de moi! I surprise myself speaking with measured impoliteness to the virulent little usher, who for ten days has kept a crowd of irritable people, drawn from all quarters of the earth, at bay before the doors of the registry. *Il y a quelqu'un qui se moque de moi!* I repeat, waving a piece of paper with a blue-pencilled number on it, the gift of this same *pion*, when last we met and I tried, with the strength of ten young men and twenty American Amazons behind me, to plant my foot on the threshold before the door was closed in our faces. The door had closed. Then, thanks either to the supreme mournfulness of our protest or to some countercommand from the dignitaries within, it had opened an inch and a handful of scraps of paper had been distributed between the most vindictive of the mob. And now I was to realize the value of a scrap of paper.

It had more than I supposed. At sight of it, my little Cerberus relaxed his defence, cringing before the frail symbol of officialdom, and in I walked to seal my fate as member of the University of Paris. The authorities were, as usual, the blandest people in the world. One of them handed me a rough little *carnet* with his signature and my name and photograph, and I came away to begin one more spell of university life.

Reader, your patience will be spent. How can I persuade you of the justice of these lamentations, when on the threshold of middle-age I persist in the habit of sampling academic *mœurs*? The truth is simply that hope springs eternal. It is also that perennially, just as I settle down to another year's routine, the desire comes to set out, to slip away and watch Autumn ripening somewhere, anywhere in France. But for this flimsy temptation an excuse must be found. I am to take a doctorate at Paris. Patience! you shall have finished that story and forgotten it, before I get that doctorate.

One good lecture before I die! Perhaps after all, this last escapade was prompted by so naïve a wish, nurtured by the fame of the versatile Faguet and the combative Brunetière, deities of my youth.

Now to hear their successors!

But alas, had I outgrown the expectancy of youth? Or was it simply that the persistent bevy of American beauties had to be cajoled, placated, perhaps even instructed, in as effortless a manner as was possible? Numbers again? Down at any rate from their pedestals fell one after another of the high gods whose oracles I had read for half a life-time with such remote and confident respect.

Even the exceptions were disquieting. One of the most respectable attracted large audiences weekly to a dismal amphitheatre. I attended for six months, picked up numerous facts about forbears and milieux before the famous 'moment' arrived when, with the apt connivance of circumstance, nothing but the subject of these discourses could have been produced from the obedient womb of time. The prospect was too painfully deterministic. I fled before the inevitable.

Everywhere it was the same. With unvaried rigidity of method they were perpetually setting the scene, but never getting to the first act. Or rather, to be just, for they were prodigiously honest workers, their business *was* to set the scene. And to set the scene was a matter of excavations. Rousseau, for instance, had apparently no connection with a contemporary discussion in which all the world outside the Sorbonne was more or less keenly interested. Rousseau was merely the last of a chain of facts, of which it was much more exciting to seek the first, whether that were the link in the first watch-chain made in Geneva or the biological Missing Link itself, the which I am persuaded most Professors of the Faculté des Lettres would have given their chairs to discover. And why not?

Facts were being unearthed, of course, and opinions corrected. But the bias of system had produced a fear of interpretation, an indifference to general ideas, an avoidance of judgements, an innocence of taste, which were really disconcerting. Impressionism had gone too far, certainly. Yet chronology aside, what is the value of a literary fact completely divorced from the impression it produces? In the last resort it was one method standardized for another liquidated.

One wondered whether the array of facts was not at times a mask. One became alarmed at the prospect of seeing the man himself emerge. What kind of observation would he make, if cornered,

upon what an antiquated person like myself called literature? There was no assurance.

But what if this brilliant breastplate of hard facts were donned over a sensitive soul, forced to confront a *cours public* in an age of iron? What would he be like in a seminar? There was at least one professor *en chaire*, not a teacher of literature, who had a way of his own and was good to hear. I gave him a chance. But when, following the custom, the doors were locked upon us, a ghost from the past took his place. This agile, loquacious little man produced a large copy-book and went on from where he had left off, turning down a corner when the bell rang, ready for next time.

A more novel experience was reserved for a friend who, having ventured into the private class of a revered Renaissance scholar, found that he had modestly arrived with a box of *fiches*. These he read out item by item, root by root, as if he were dictating an etymological dictionary!

O tempora, o mores! Had no one in France the gift of tongues? I was about to exchange my dreams of eloquence for a wreath to be laid at the foot of Hugo's statue in the *cour*, when the kind fortune that had never failed me *in extremis* recalled an incident in my first trip to Paris.

Keen to impress me with the intellectual splendours of her country, the excellent *dame* with whom I stayed had insisted that I must hear Bergson at the Collège de France. I have told how I had arrived an hour before the lecture to find the largest room in the building packed with a crowd that overflowed into the corridors, through which the philosopher had to insinuate himself in order to ascend the *chaire*. The mob closed in after him and the more stalwart disposed themselves like a nimbus of tousled seraphs around his person, as he sat to speak. I heard nothing of the *causerie;* but by shameless manoeuvres I succeeded in gaining a glimpse of gestures through a glass door at the back of the room. They were suave and persuasive. It was several years since they had ceased to mesmerise that audience. But the Collège de France remained. Could their influence still hang about the place?

Next morning I arrived an hour in advance to hear Abel Lefranc. I learnt that he was to lecture in the shabby but illustrious *salle* where I had observed the fluid movements of Bergson. But there was as yet no sign of an audience. Nor were signs much more abundant

when I took up a position in the middle of the room an hour later. As the clock struck in came the scholar at one door while a sniffling old lady entered at another, and the lecture began.

Rabelais!—The heavens opened and on the parched plains of life-long anticipation there began to fall the first fresh drops of scholarly eloquence. Voluble enthusiasm, ample gesticulation put at the service of extensive learning produced the miracle. The robust figure of the recalcitrant monk, the learned doctor of Montpellier and Lyons rose before me, no longer an abstraction, connecting certain facts or resuming certain tendencies, but a lively, authentic person of jollity and genius.

Balm in Gilead! I emerged into the courtyard to consult dates for future lectures. Six more! My heart sank. A miracle had happened. Could the same magician perform seven? Doubt fell like a bolt from the blue—doubt and an idea. He had given me a glimpse of the Renaissance. Here in the Luxembourg was Spring!

A week ago had come two superb days. Hardly a bud was showing yet one felt the branches were ready to burst. During the heavy showers, the hail and thunders of an April week, they had burst, and today with fair weather there was more green than black showing. But what caught my eye were great blobs of cream, hovering like edible snowflakes in and out, through, between and all over the black network of intertwined boughs. What a sight, when the candle-like blossoms would appear! But should I wait to see them?

That night a lumbering *rapide* making for the Midi bore in the corner of an empty compartment a middle-aged truant in quest of his youth.

Avoiding the steps of the Duomo as too reminiscent of Renan at the Acropolis, I climbed to the terrace of San Miniato for the vision which I had felt immanent since I left Paris. Established above that miraculous panorama, lo! I said to myself in language unused since childhood. And like Banquo's review of kings, there passed before my gaze the forms of my teachers wistfully trying, as spiritualists say, to get through.

What had they given me with their long solicitude? Religion? Philosophy? Ideals? A theory? A technique? A tendency? An orientation? . . .

The questions broadened into vaguer abstractions and lost themselves in chimes from below. The graceful city stood out,

untrammelled and precise in the waning light. There genius had wrought a wealth of beauty now at my feet. Suddenly I realized the happy ineffectualness, the innocence of my education. It had scratched the surface of a few things. It had worried like Martha over the rudiments of many. It had left realities everywhere intact.

In an ecstasy of gratitude for its innocuous triviality, I descended gravely into the Florentine dusk.

DATE DUE